Sit Down and Shut Up!

My Many Misadventures in Public Education

ROGER WONG

PAGE PUBLISHING, INC.
New York, NY

First originally published by Page Publishing, Inc. 2016

ISBN 978-1-68289-750-8 (pbk)
ISBN 978-1-68289-751-5 (digital)

Printed in the United States of America

Contents

Introduction

Oh, no! Not another book about public education! Haven't we already been thoroughly saturated with these kinds of books, not to mention the prominence of this topic in the newspapers and on TV. We don't want to hear another word about ineffective teachers, out-of-control students, and out-of-touch administrators. We already know about pathetic student test scores, unqualified teachers, and fatty school lunches. School buses in need of repair, controversial teacher evaluations, and teacher accountability are getting to be some pretty tiresome subjects. And please don't tell me about having to raise taxes to support a mediocre educational system or how textbooks and technology in schools are outdated. *Please! Stop!* Okay, okay, okay, time out. Let me assure you right now that this book is *not* about any of these things.

Now, the education of today's youth is certainly *not* a laughing matter. Yet many therapists will tell you that you will be a much happier and better adjusted person if you can learn to laugh at yourself, your mistakes, and your life in general. Humor is a funny thing, and I mean that literally! The source of a lot of humor comes from negative things, like embarrassing situations, relationships gone awry, racism, and ignorance—you know, the things that happen to you that were not funny at the time but hilarious afterward. It's all about perspective.

So I think it's fitting that there should finally be something written about teaching and education that is a bit more lighthearted and shows, amidst all the current seriousness surrounding the profession, that there are actually some funny and extraordinary—and maybe, shocking—things that happen at the grassroots level in schools that are not usually expressed openly. In fact, some may label some of these things that happen behind the scenes as inappropriate, surprising, or even disgusting. But they happened to me, nonetheless. And it wouldn't surprise me if teachers across the nation had similar experiences.

If you have ever wondered what school teachers *really* think about parents, students, administrators, and other teachers, this is the book for you. It's definitely not neat and pretty. And it may not fit into your preconceived notions about the profession of teaching. In fact, the incidences I will describe in this book may be interpreted as unbecoming of teachers. Some readers may think that teachers should not be saying, doing, or thinking these things. But teachers are human beings too, and these kinds of things do happen, and occur, in many other professions as well.

The incidences disclosed in this book are all frank and honest. The chronology of some of the events has been rearranged to accommodate better story flow, and there are some minor and rare embellishments. But the core happenings did, in fact, occur. To protect people's privacy, I have used fictitious names.

Most of the narratives detailed in this book should sound familiar to many teachers. What teacher has not, for example, had that troublesome, jerk student who made their classroom life miserable? What teacher has not had comical class occurrences or tried to help a student but couldn't? What teacher has not developed meaningful friendships with fellow teachers? Sometimes it may even be romantic. What teacher has not, at one time or another, had evil, sinful thoughts about certain students or staff members? What teacher has not lied to a student in order to save face, or made at least one silly social or academic mistake in class?

I hope this book will resonate with most teachers. It might make you smile, knowing you are not alone in the sometimes-crazy world of education. What has happened to me, in thirty-four years of teaching, has happened to many teachers in one form or another. The names, places, and dates are different, but the basic experience is the same. I'm going to tell you simply, and in my own words, about some of my more memorable adventures during my lengthy teaching career, and hopefully you will be enlightened and entertained along the way.

For you, readers, who are not teachers, this book will be a window into the real world of the teacher. Many of you may think you already have a clear idea of what it's like to teach because you have attended schools yourself. But I'll bet you'll uncover a number of insights, and realize many unexpected truths about education, from the teacher's perspective. We all grew up, as children, observing our parents, yet we really didn't fully understand what parenting was all about until we became parents ourselves. This is because both groups (parent and child) had undisclosed secrets. They each embraced a virtual cache of confidential information that was not shared with the other group. The same circumstances exist with respect to the teacher and student.

So get ready to be educated yet again. And along the way, you may also be shocked, humored, saddened, surprised, and maybe even angered. This, my friends, is my thirty-four-year adventure as a public school teacher.

Chapter 1

Knowing When to Teach

Teacher: Okay, class, what do you want to be when you grow up? Johnny?

Johnny: I wanna be a billionaire, go to expensive clubs, take the best babe with me, and buy her a Ferrari, a mansion, and an infinite VISA card.

(The teacher, shocked, decides not to give importance to Johnny's inappropriate answer and continues.)

Teacher: And what do you want to be, Suzy?

Suzy: I want to be Johnny's babe.

I didn't know I was going to be a teacher until it was almost too late. In fact, the decision, for me, wasn't revealed until the end of my junior year at college. This was pretty unusual. Most teachers had already made this decision prior to entering college, if not much earlier. Unbeknownst to me, *when* you knew you wanted to be a teacher was an important question asked at job interviews. The idea among educational administrators was that the earlier in life you knew you wanted to teach, the better teacher you would become. The earlier in life you knew this, the more motivated, excited, and passionate you were about the teaching profession. The reasoning was that if you dreamed of becoming a teacher for a very long time, then actually fulfilling that dream would be absolutely marvelous. You'd be so excited to do the job. So the answer to this question was crucial to the chances of you being hired. I'm not sure, but I think someone did a study and found out that the really good, effective teachers were the ones who knew they wanted to teach at a young age. So I guess this philosophy makes some sort of sense—on the other hand, maybe not.

Do you remember back in early elementary school when your teacher talked about future careers and asked the class about what they wanted to be when they grew up? The question was usually proposed on that delightful day of the school year labeled "Career Day." Sometimes this day involved media presentations about interesting careers or live speakers who enthusiastically narrated engrossing stories about their wonderful jobs. It almost always involved classroom participation as well. The teacher wanted to know, with much manufactured interest, what each of her students had in mind as a future career. The conversation, in Mrs. Smith's second grade class, would go something like this:

> Mrs. Smith: Good morning, class! Okay, settle down now… Please, students, let me have your attention…I'm waiting for you to be quiet…Okay, now, I *said* I'm waiting…Dang it! *Shut up!* Okay, thanks! Today is a very special day. Today is Career Day! [*There's muffled golf clapping and some unsure yeah responses from three or four students.*] It's never too early to think about what you want to be when you grow up. Let's start by going around the room so every student can tell the class what they want to be. You're seven years old, and it's important you think about your future! Jimmy, let's start with you!
>
> Jimmy: Mrs. Smith, I want to be an astronaut!

Mrs. Smith: Great, Jimmy! That's wonderful! How about you, Sally?

Sally: I'm going to be a professional ballet dancer! I started taking lessons last week, and my ballet teacher tells me I'm really good at it.

Mrs. Smith: Outstanding! And what do you want to be, Billy?

Billy: I'm going to be a professional baseball player! Last season I played third base for my Pee Wee team. We came in second place in the whole league! And my Dad told me that if I keep up the good work I can really go far.

Mrs. Smith: Wow! Awesome! And, Roger, what about you?

Roger: I want to be a teacher!

Mrs. Smith (*after awkward silence*): That's just…[*more awkward silence*]…really nice, Roger. [*Giggles from students*] Gee, Roger, can't you think of a higher goal than that?

Okay, Mrs. Smith didn't really say that last line, but that's what she was thinking. A seven-year-old should be dreaming of something bigger, better, and more exotic than being a teacher. It's sad for a kid this early in life to have such low expectations. In fact, it's sad when anyone of any age has low expectations for themselves. For example, I've heard college freshmen say things like, "I'm so excited! I'm going to major in philosophy, move to Hawaii, and live on the beach free!" or a high school senior saying, "If I can just pass Mr. Donahue's basic math class, I'll graduate. Then I can move out of the house, work at Wendy's, and get my studio apartment."

Now, don't get me wrong. There's nothing inherently wrong with majoring in philosophy (okay, I guess there is!), living in Hawaii, or working at Wendy's. But it just seems like these people are selling themselves short, just like the second-grader who wants to be a teacher, instead of an astronaut, professional baseball player, or ballet dancer. When you are seven, you should be dreaming big, and wanting to be a teacher is a little on the small side.

Anyway, and fortunately, I was never asked in the interview for my first teaching position about *when* I knew I wanted to be a teacher. Because if I had been asked, I would have been compelled to tell the truth, which would ultimately and inevitably end with me never being hired:

> Administrator: Mr. Wong, we really think you may be perfect for the current teaching position we have open. But we have one more question. When did you first realize you wanted to be a teacher?
>
> Me: Well, I was going to college and majoring in sociology (second only to philosophy in uselessness), and by the time I was at the end of my junior year, I began wondering what the hell am I going to do for a living. I totally enjoyed sociology and was quite fascinated by its many interesting topics, but when I realized my occupational options were limited, I sort of started to panic. Okay, I thought, I could be a social "worker." No, that sounded like too much "work." I could go into researching group behavior through a university, but I'd need at least a master's degree in sociology to qualify for that, and I'm sort of broke right now. Then it hit me. I could be a social studies teacher! I might have to take a few extra classes, but think of the advantages! You get three months off in the summer, plus extended Christmas and other holiday breaks. You are working inside a building, so you don't have to worry about inclement weather, and although I hear the pay isn't so good, people have told me teachers have pretty good health benefits.
>
> Administrator: Huh…all right, Mr. Wong. [*Then an awkward, uncomfortable silence accompanied with darting glances amongst the interview team.*] We actually have a few more candidates to interview. It was a pleasure talking with you.

I have to imagine this same interview team hiring someone who said they knew they wanted to be a teacher very, very early in life:

First Teacher Candidate

Administrator: Thanks for sharing your answers today. Our last question is: when did you know you wanted to be a teacher?

First candidate: I knew I wanted to be a teacher in ninth grade. I had this wonderful, kind, and caring science teacher. I'll never forget him. He was so energetic and motivating. I knew then that I wanted to teach.

Administrator: Great answer. We'll give you a call once we have interviewed the remaining two candidates.

Second Teacher Candidate

Administrator: Thanks for your thought-provoking answers. Just one more question. When did you know you wanted to be a teacher?

Second candidate: I knew in first grade I wanted to be a teacher. My first grade teacher was Mrs. Dupree, and she was totally inspiring. She made every story she read to us exciting and every assignment fun. She made such a positive impact on my young life. I remember distinctly saying to myself that I want to be just like Mrs. Dupree. I want to mold minds, positively influence youngsters, and have fun doing it. I want to be a teacher!

Administrator: Wow! Wonderful answer! We only have one more candidate to interview, but you can expect a call from us later this afternoon.

Third Teacher Candidate

Administrator: Okay, I must admit your answers thus far have been quite impressive, but we have one more important question. When did you know you wanted to be a teacher?

Third candidate: I knew I wanted to be a teacher when I was two months old! I very clearly, unmistakably, and positively remember my mother flailing her arms in front of me and making sounds, sort of like how the adults talk on those Charlie Brown cartoons. Somehow I figured out she was trying to tell me to do what she was doing, that is, flailing her arms. So I started flailing my arms. My mother screamed with joy and called my dad over to witness the teaching miracle she had performed. I'll never forget the look of happiness and pride on my mom's face. I knew then that there was something magical and wonderful about teaching. And I wanted to experience it. That's when I definitely knew I wanted to be a teacher!

Administrator: Unbelievable! Fantastic! *You are hired!*

So needless to say, I decided to become a teacher pretty late in life, especially compared to candidate no. 3, and compared to most teachers in general. And yes, I entered the field with less than the best of intentions. I will fully admit that. But after a successful thirty-four-year career in education, it worked out. Many things in life have a tendency to work themselves out. Some, however, not only work themselves out, but become the best decision in a person's life. And this was the case with me.

Chapter 2

Teaching Is Not for Everyone

Teaching is a complicated endeavor. Not everyone can teach, even though they may think they can. My sister taught math at a high school for thirty-seven years. She married a man who was a geologist. When my sister would occasionally complain about some aspect of the teaching profession, her husband would simply dismiss it. He could not fathom why teaching could be so difficult. After all, you merely announce the assignment, sit back and watch the students work, and grade the papers at your convenience. What's so hard about that? But his own job was somewhat seasonal, and a bit hard on his back, so he decided to give himself a break and become a teacher. The first step to becoming a teacher was to take a university class where you visit a handful of schools over the course of a semester, observe the teachers and students, and maybe write a few papers about what you saw. But for reasons that were never divulged, he unexpectedly quit. He either discovered his personality didn't fit teaching or that teaching was way more difficult than he had previously thought. And I think the latter was a bit more accurate.

Also, Tony Danza, the TV star of the 1980s sitcoms *Taxi* and *Who's the Boss*, had always dreamed of being a teacher. So at age sixty, he decided to finally fulfill his dream and later wrote a book about his experiences. He completed the *Teach for America* program and found himself teaching tenth grade English at an inner city school in Philadelphia, the city where he grew up. He taught one "block" class, consisting of two hours per day, for one year. After discovering the difficulties and demands of this "dream" job, he states, "I now see America's educators as heroes who deserve our wholehearted respect and support" (Danza 2012, 258). Keep in mind that if Mr. Danza would have been a full-time teacher, at least two other classes would have been added to his rigorous schedule, making his teaching experience even more difficult and demanding. Mr. Danza admitted he was not the best student, nor the best behaved, when he was in high school. And after learning the brutal truth about teaching himself, he amply titles his book *I'd Like to Apologize to Every Teacher I Ever Had!*

So teaching is not for everyone out there. There are so many factors that make teaching tough, and briefly, here are some of them:

1) Students

Pupil: I don't think I deserved a zero on this test.
Teacher: I agree, but that's the lowest mark I could give you.

Everyone knows, because they have been in school themselves, that students can create some serious headaches for teachers. Maybe you were one of them! Anyway, schools drawing from poverty-stricken inner city areas are filled with students who are behind academically and burdened with a myriad of issues at home. This, obviously, carries over to the classroom and makes teaching and connecting with kids much more challenging. But rich kids have problems too, and these problems affect their classroom behavior just as much as the poor kid. The divorce of parents, for example, does not discriminate based on income, nor does drug addiction, verbal or physical abuse, neglect, or a multitude of other problems. So just because you landed a teaching job on the wealthy side of town does not mean you're in for cooperative, motivated, happy, brilliant students.

I taught at schools that drew from a middle-class base, so I have seen and dealt with every kind of student out there. I have to admit, most of the students, most of the time, at least, tried to be cooperative. But several times a month, I would get student outbursts, misbehaviors (small and large), and/or aggressive behaviors. For example, my colleague and friend at school, who taught social studies, kicked a kid out of class for inappropriate language and failure to follow instructions. While this student was sitting in the vice principal's office, he decided to use the time constructively by improving his writing skills. He composed the following, which he quickly placed in the teacher's school mailbox:

[I've given it to you exactly the way it was written, except for the teacher's and vice principal's real names.]

Mr. Hatfield,

Yo, you needa get yo fat ass on da treadmill

FUCK YOU Mr. Hatfield you are a mother fucking fat bitch,

If you ever fuckin send me out to Dr. Lock's office for some small ass shit...

YOUR ASS WILL END UP WET UP, with a cap up yo ass.

Shit NIGGA yo MOMMA probably died from givin' ass birth.

Your ass look like you are pregnant wit twins and shit.

That's why yo fat ass gotta eat by yourself b/c everyone else know dat your ass is gonna eat their fuckin' food.

I'da shoot your fuckin' ass for some shit like that, that you did.

I'm happy that you're ugly; fat ass Mother is dead

And I will go piss on her grave so that her dead ass can taste, then I hope that your fucking

fat ass can go to hell and plus your dead ass Mom
can suck MY DICK BITCH.

Eatin' up all the food and shit. And your fat
ass is fatter that all the other teachers, haven't you
noticed that, you FAT FUCK ASS NIGGA. Go chase
the twinky bitch.

You are fucking up my life.

Wow! This student was in eighth grade. He was suspended from
school for a week. So no matter what kind of school a teacher may
find himself or herself at, students have the potential to ruin your day.

2) Parents

The second-grader wasn't getting good marks at school.
One day, he tapped his teacher on the shoulder and said, "I don't
want to scare you, Mrs. Appleton, but my daddy told me that if
I don't get better grades, somebody is going to get a spanking."

Part of your job as an educator is to contact and work with parents,
hopefully as a team, to maximize the student's educational experience. You'll see parents at open house toward the beginning of the
year, where the focus is explaining the curriculum. Most, if not all
schools, have required parent conferences, sometimes several times
during the year. At these conferences, teachers meet with individual
parents to discuss the student's academic progress and what the student needs to do to improve.

Furthermore, some districts are now suggesting, or requiring,
teachers to contact parents on a regular basis via e-mail, phone, or
website, so the parents know what is going on in class that day or
week and what assignments they are working on and when they are
due. Teachers must also contact parents if there are any discipline
issues with their child.

All of these contacts with parents take a lot of hours.
Communicating with parents is one of the many time-consuming
elements the teacher must complete within their already-crazy sched-

ule. This is one factor that causes a teacher's workweek to end up fifty-plus hours long. And I know many teachers who put in even more time than this.

Also, speaking of parents, a teacher will come across an unreasonable parent every once in a while because some parents place the blame for their child's academic shortcomings on the teacher, when this is rarely the truth. There's a cartoon that demonstrates this point nicely. In one scene, a disgruntled dad is standing next to his son who is showing him a D on his report card. The dad angrily asks him why he got a D. The son's head is down, and he's clearly embarrassed as he's taking full responsibility for the poor mark. This scene is labeled "Then." The next scene shows the same dad and son, with a D on his report card, standing in front of the teacher's desk. The teacher's head is down. The dad indignantly asks the teacher why he gave his son a poor grade. This scene is labeled "Now." In other words, the blame for the poor academic performance has shifted from the student to the teacher. Of course, not all parents have this posture, but it certainly seems much more common now compared to 1979, when I first started teaching.

So dealing delicately with irrational, kid-protecting parents can be a very frustrating part of the job. I've had more than one conversation with a parent that went something like this (what I *really* wanted to say is in brackets):

Parent: I see you gave my son a D. Why's that?

Me: Well, let me take a quick peek at the grade book... It looks like he's missing a couple assignments, and he didn't do very well on his five-paragraph paper, which was worth a lot of points.

[Your son earned a D because he's a below-average student, which is what D means, sir.]

Parent: My son showed me his five-paragraph essay. I read it, and I thought it was great.

Me: Well, there were certain writing criteria he needed to have, and some of those were not present in his paper.

[*You* thought it was great? Are *you* the teacher, or I?]

Parent: What criteria? It looked fine to me.

Me: If I remember correctly, he didn't have a thesis statement in his introductory paragraph, which is crucial. And he failed to restate his main ideas in his concluding paragraph.

[Why don't you come in and teach the class yourself, you know-it-all.]

Parent: Okay, fine. I just don't think he deserved a D. Your grade has caused him to be stressed out. Because of you, he may not be eligible to play for the basketball team now.

Me: Well, I'm really sorry about that, but if he works to his potential next quarter, I'm sure he'll raise his grade significantly.

[Can I take a picture of you, to use you as the poster parent for enabling behaviors?]

Parent: Okay, but I just don't think you are being fair.

Me: I'm so sorry, sir…Have a great day!

[Eat me, asshole!]

3) Administrators

"Isn't the principal a dummy?" said a boy to a girl.
"Well, do you know who I am?" said the girl.
"No," replied the boy.
"Well, I'm the principal's daughter."
"And do you know who I am?" asks the boy.
"No," she replied.
"Thank goodness!" said the boy with a sigh of relief.

Then there are your bosses, the administrators. Every school has a principal who runs the school. He or she hires, begins the process of firing, decides who teaches what, evaluates teachers, and deals with parents, the community, and the nonteaching staff—such as custo-dians, counselors, lunchroom help, teacher's aides, and the vice prin-cipals. The VPs are also bosses over the teachers. But their main job is student discipline. They may also evaluate teachers and help the principal with his or her duties. Being a principal or VP is admittedly a demanding, difficult job. You are often caught in between conflict-ing groups. For example, the district superintendent may require you to implement a policy you know is unpopular with the teachers and staff, but you pretty much have to do it anyway or risk the security of your own paycheck. You may also find yourself caught between a parent and a teacher over a discipline issue with a student. You have to make a decision, and usually, that decision will not sit right with either the parent or the teacher, or even both. Your time requirements are hefty as well. You must attend PTA meetings, community meet-ings, and the school's sporting events, plays, or concerts. The other dilemma surrounding principals is that, in many cases, they have not taught for a long time—or maybe *never* taught. At the middle school I taught at, one of the Vice-principals who was evaluating teachers had never taught at all. She had been a school counselor prior to get-ting her administrative credentials and being hired.

It seemed to me sort of ridiculous that she was evaluating teach-ers. So sometimes teachers get quite perturbed with the administra-tor's assessments of their teaching. They come into the classroom a few times during the year and expect to know what's going on, believ-ing they know more than the teacher, even though they may not have taught for twenty years, or not taught at all. How can they possibly evaluate a teacher who may have had years and years of experience and has been with the students all year? Sort of ridiculous, if you ask me! Also, the administrator's academic background may have been in history, let's say, which would logically make it difficult for them to assess a science teacher, without the knowledge of that particular sub-ject matter. Anyway, my point is that sometimes, an administrator can be a sharp thorn in the teacher's behind. In fact, I was shocked, after teaching for a few years, to learn that the principal's main job description was to "support teachers." I had previously thought their job was to give teachers a bad time and make them feel inadequate.

Of course, not all principals are detrimental to a teacher's effectiveness. I was fortunate to work for a principal for sixteen years who was very supportive, kind, and knowledgeable. He proved to me that principals don't have to be assholes and that there is such a thing as outstanding leadership.

4) Workload

To all employees, new incentive plan!
Work, or be fired.

Being a teacher is a salaried position, which means you get paid a set amount, no matter how many hours you put in. The school day is normally about seven hours long. But I can't think of too many teachers who go home with nothing to do. There are lesson plans to write, papers to grade, meetings to attend, lessons to reflect upon, student needs to assess, supplies to gather (and possibly buy with your own money), grades to enter into the gradebook, parents to contact, and teachers to collaborate with. If you volunteer for a school sport or activity—which is, in some schools, a requirement—you have to take care of all those aforementioned duties later, like in the evenings at home or early before school the next day.

The workload is particularly heavy in your first few years of teaching. After all, you're new. You really don't know that much about teaching at this early stage. The rookie mistakes you inevitably make may cause you to put in even more time. This might be why the turnover rate for teachers is quite high, with the average teacher lasting only five years. In fact, I came pretty close to quitting my first year of teaching, after being exposed to the outlandish time commitment, as well as the other frustrations explained in this chapter, and my own lack of effectiveness being the green teacher I was!

Also, during the last ten years or so, the workload of teachers has increased due to the many educational "reforms" that have been thrust upon teachers. The current societal feeling is that teachers are mostly to blame for students who do not learn. As a result, there are a myriad of ridiculous reforms that are actually detrimental to student learning and add extra time to the teacher's already-full workload. Never mind the parents, their peers, their socioeconomic status, or their family problems. These things, of course, have no impact on learning! So it is the belief of these so-called reformers that a teacher should be able to take a homeless, starving, neglected, drug-addicted gang-banger and make him pass a rather difficult state test, or shame on the teacher!

It may sound like I hate teaching, but I don't. I'm just laying out some of the difficulties of the job. Actually, I'm so glad I found teaching and fell into my predestined niche. Although surrounded by the frustration explained above, I actually found teaching to be rather easy, for the most part. I guess I was just programmed correctly for this kind of occupation, or learned enough to get real comfortable with it. I can remember that there were more days when I rather looked forward to getting up in the morning and going to school. I looked forward to the day's lessons. I was eager to get to school and develop rapport with the kids. I daresay I have been a pretty lucky guy. I doubt too many people in the workforce can say they actually love their jobs, like me.

Chapter 3

Liar, Liar, Pants on Fire!

I am different than George Washington; I have a
higher, grander standard of principle. Washington
could not lie. I can lie, but I won't.

—Mark Twain

In order to survive as a respected teacher, you need to occasionally lie to your students. And it wouldn't hurt to have some thes-
pian talents as well. After all, teachers are human beings with a
variety of activities they indulge in after school and on week-
ends. The problem is that, as a teacher, it's better for everyone
involved if your students respect you, hold you in high esteem, and
regard your actions as examples of how to carry oneself properly. To
this end, they need to believe that you are morally impeccable, along
the lines of Mother Theresa or Mahatma Gandhi. They also need
to believe you are way more knowledgeable about the subject you
are teaching than they are, and you need to drill into the students'
heads the absolute importance of the material you are teaching. The
information, the students should know, is crucial to their future lives

as successful citizens of America. Consequently, you must sometimes tell little (and sometimes big) fibs to your students.

I taught US history in high school for more than six years. History and social studies classes, in general, tend to be perceived by many as the least valuable classes in public schools. Thus, over the years, districts have slowly dwindled down the social studies requirements. The truth is that, unless you are going to be a history teacher, or you find yourself on Jeopardy with one of the categories being "World War II" or "Presidents Beginning with the Letter *R*," you probably will never use the information again. Now, if you are a social studies teacher reading this, calm down! Let us just admit that we have to try harder to convince our students that the information is important. I can remember a conversational exchange I had with a high school student when we were reviewing the correct answers on a test they had taken the day before. It unfolded like this:

Me: Okay, the answer to question 36 is "Trench Warfare." Does anyone have a question about this? Bruce, you have a question?

Bruce: Yes, Mr. Wong, sorry to get a little off subject here, but I was wondering why we need to know this stuff, like the fact that World War I started in 1914, which, by the way, I got wrong on the test. I am really good at fixing cars and plan to be a mechanic. I just don't see where this information will help me.

Me: (*I turn toward his desk slowly, with eyebrows raised and in a voice that is doing all it can to mask my indignation*): Whether you are a mechanic, engineer, doctor, lawyer, or a darn bum on the street, you *need* to know history. History is about *your* past and explains who you are. For Pete's sake, do you know the name of the illness that people have who do not know their past? It's called *amnesia*! And it's a certifiable mental condition. *Do you want to graduate from high school with a mental illness?*

Bruce: Well, huh…I guess not, Mr. Wong.

Me: I didn't think so. It's my job to make sure each and every one of you sitting in class today become knowledgeable, productive citizens of this great country of ours. Now, let's get back to the test review.

Wow! I really deserved an academy award for that one!

I can remember another occasion where a student was offering up some friendly chat right before class was about to begin. In order to keep my respect as a teacher intact, I had to lie again. The friendly little exchange went like this, with the *truth* outlined in brackets.

Student: Hi, Mr. Wong! How are you today?

Me: Oh, just great! And thanks for asking. [I feel terrible!]

Student: What did you do over the weekend?

Me: Well, I finished reading a really interesting book on Abraham Lincoln and took my wife out to dinner. [I got totally smashed Saturday night and needed all day Sunday to recover.]

Student: Gee, our family went out to dinner too. What restaurant did you go to?

Me: You know that vegetarian restaurant downtown? We go there a couple times a month. The food is so refreshingly healthy. [I didn't go out to dinner. I was either drunk or nursing a hangover.]

Student: Mr. Wong, I've lived here all my life, and I don't think there's a vegetarian restaurant downtown.

Me: Well, it may be just outside of town. (Hurriedly) Okay, everyone, let's get in your seats and take out your notebooks! Hurry, the bell rang!

      [I lied to you about the vegetarian restaurant. I was laid up most of the weekend. And I wish you'd stop asking me questions about my personal life, you suck-up.]

It's really embarrassing if a student knows more than you about the subject you are teaching. The bachelor's or master's degree you earned from the university does not necessarily guarantee you are smarter than your students. Most teachers will tell you that the best way to learn a subject is to teach it. So the real learning for the teacher begins when they first start to teach.

I graduated from the University of Washington in 1979 with a BA in Sociology, a BA in History, and a BA in Education. Pretty impressive, right? Not really. My first job right out of the university was teaching Pacific Northwest history and language arts, both to ninth-graders. I'll never forget how skillfully I was able to convince the principal who interviewed me that I could successfully teach language arts:

Principal: Okay, Mr. Wong, I see here that you seem to be very qualified to teach history, but this position involves one section of ninth grade language arts. Do you think you could handle that?

Me: Huh, sure.

Principal: Okay, great! We'll see you on Monday.

No joke! That's how the interview went down, and I was hired! Nowadays, prospective teaching candidates must show they are "qualified" to teach the subject(s) they are hired for. However, many teachers find themselves teaching subjects outside their academic areas for a variety of reasons. And even if you are teaching within your so-called specialty, you can still run into students more knowledgeable than you about certain aspects of your curriculum. When I taught US history to juniors, there always seemed to be a student (without exception, male) who had a special interest in something, like World War II aircraft, and could tell you *anything* you wanted to know about it. So as I'm teaching World War II, he'd raise his hand and give a dissertation about World War II aircraft to the entire class. I just sort of winked at him as he was spewing out this information for a good ten minutes while I'm pretending to already know what he's saying.

Anyway, you don't want the students to think you are dumb. So once again, you sometimes have to lie in order to keep the student's respect. And when I found myself teaching ninth grade language arts, I was really thankful for a textbook to read a day ahead of the class. I recall, vividly, trying to teach the parts of speech to these ninth graders and was proud to make it through all of the parts of speech without too many boo-boos on my part. Or so I thought…

Student: Mr. Wong, are we done with the parts of speech?

Me: We sure are! And I'm proud of all of you. It's not the most interesting topic, but you guys hung in there, and we got it done.

Student: But, Mr. Wong, there are *eight* parts of speech, and you only taught us seven. The eighth part of speech is interjections.

Me: Well…huh…yes, it is. You said the eighth part of speech is interjections? Yes, well, that part of speech is the least important one, and we don't have time to cover it. We need to move on and learn next about sentence structure.

Student: Okay, Mr. Wong. But I just thought I would mention it.

Me: I *really* appreciate you mentioning it. You *and* I were the only ones in class who knew that. You have definitely earned a gold star today! (*Student displays an enormous smile and looks around at other students with an aura of superiority.*)

When it's all put in perspective, students do learn a lot from their teachers and will move into the real world ready, willing, and able. They don't need to know that their teachers have lied to them every once in a while. Like I've mentioned, sometimes teachers *must* lie! For instance, I've had students who, for whatever bizarre reason, take a liking to me. For some unknown reason, they want to be like me. They look up to me and want to emulate me. As a result, for all I know, I may have saved him (let's call him Tony) from imminent danger or maybe prevented him from becoming an alcoholic:

Tony: Hey, Pat, it's Friday night! What's on the agenda?

Pat: We're going to have a great time tonight!

Tony: Really, why?

Pat: Don't tell anyone, but I stole a bottle of whiskey from my parent's liquor cabinet. Come on, Tony, let's go to the gully and get wasted!!

Tony: No, Pat, I will not do that.

Pat: Why not? It's going to be soooo cool!

Tony: Because Mr. Wong would *not* do that!

Pat: What the hell? Who cares about Mr. Wong, you stinking idiot!

Tony: Well, I do. You can go without me.

Pat: Okay, you loser. You're going to miss out on a great time...By the way, what are you going to do tonight?

Tony: I'm going to go home and read a book about Abraham Lincoln.

Chapter 4

Show and Terror

I don't want to achieve immortality
through my work.
I want to achieve immortality by not dying.
I'm not afraid to die. I just don't want
to be around when it happens.

—Woody Allen

When I was in school, I hated giving speeches. They terrified me. I was one of those students who were extra cognizant about what others thought of me. The idea of stuttering, forgetting what I wanted to say, or having some sort of wardrobe malfunction kept me up most of the night before the speech. I would rather have my molars pulled out without the assistance of novocaine than be caught in front of the class with my fly open, my shirt tag hanging out, or lettuce visible between my two front teeth. I was clinically paranoid about it. My elevated anxiety level the morning of the speech caused me to perspire profusely, which in turn caused more imagined embarrassment. Dripping sweat hitting the tiled classroom floor, while trying to babble through information about George

Washington, would send me bolting for the door, never to set foot in the classroom again. Oh! The mortification of facing those students would be unbearable and humiliating beyond belief!

Yes, I was quite the wreck when required to address the class. I hated and despised it. So when I became a teacher, I vowed to never require my students to give speeches. I think a lot of teachers modify their pedagogy, or their lesson plans, based on their own past depraved school experiences. This is because teachers are, in general, nice people and don't want their students to suffer as they did.

I guess it never crossed my mind that some students might actually enjoy public speaking. It seemed these peculiar students were rather low in number, though, and they didn't grumble too much about not having the opportunity to do it. The fact of the matter was that most students appreciated Mr. Wong's absence of social discomfort, public shame, and peer disgrace.

Unfortunately, when I found myself teaching tenth grade language arts in the early 1980s, "Public Communication" was a rigid and required part of the curriculum. This meant I was forced to have students give at least one speech during the semester. *Okay, fine*, I thought. But I will make it as painless as possible. They should talk about something they already know a lot about, are comfortable with, and is important to them personally. So I figured, an updated version of show-and-tell would work to ease the distress associated with such a horrid assignment. In particular, I described the speech requirements to the class this way:

"Okay, class, oral communication is an important skill to master. No matter what profession you are currently thinking about, speaking clearly to others will be greatly beneficial to you. You'll be better off in the long run if you can express yourself assertively to others, rather than conceal your opinions and thus not take advantage of all that life has to offer. So to this end, I'd like you to bring in an object from home that is very important to you and explain to the class why it is important. Make sure your presentation is between two and four minutes long. Speeches that are shorter or longer, even by one second, will be docked points. I will have a stopwatch. Therefore, when you are planning your speech, try to shoot for three minutes to avoid any timing issues. All of you have intriguing hobbies, special talents, or curious interests. I'm really looking forward to these speeches."

So on the appointed day, I took my stopwatch and grading documents and repaired to the back of the room to observe and grade their speeches. I always asked for volunteers first. If there were no volunteers, I'd simply go by the seating chart. It's curious that I'd almost always have a few volunteers right off the bat, though. Actually, when I was in school, I wanted to go first as well. My thinking was that I needed to get this over with as soon as possible, rather than suffer through the mental anguish that would be eating away at my sensibilities. On the other hand, there were maybe one or two students, out of twenty-eight, who really enjoyed this type of admonishment and volunteered because they were truly stimulated by addressing the class. It was difficult to tell these two groups apart as they raised their hands to volunteer.

The first presenter was a petite, politely mannered girl who smiled freely and proudly as she flaunted her porcelain doll given to her by her grandmother at age three. She had dressed formally solely for the occasion of this speech. As it turned out, the doll had become a prominent part of her life, as she slept with it, dithered over it, and reminisced about it upon her grandmother's passing.

Another student brought in a picture of his dog and unceremoniously began explaining about the dog's behavior and unconvincingly alluded to the dog's importance to the family. It was apparent to me that he had thrown the whole thing together at the last minute and was trying to persuade the audience, and me, that the dog was of great value. But it just didn't work. His constant silent interludes, overuse of the filler "huh…" and jittery delivery pronounced the fact that he was clearly winging it, with a rather unfortunate outcome.

Yet another student brought in his tennis racket and boorishly detailed how he was the number 1 seed on the school's tennis team. He wore his neatly pressed white tennis shorts, a perfectly white T-shirt displaying the school's name and mascot, and a fashionable light-blue headband. He looked like some pompous ass ready to play a few matches at a private, well-to-do, you-must-be-ridiculously-rich tennis club. He was sure he'd get a full-ride scholarship to UCLA or

USC and continued at length about how talented he was and how he was on track to break the school record for most single's wins. It was nothing but an exercise in self-advertisement. It did, however, meet the speech's requirements, and I couldn't dock him points just because he was an arrogant jerk.

Finally, as the speeches were winding down, a student, whom I will call Jordan, raised his hand to go next. I noticed he had brought with him some kind of unfamiliar black case. It looked like it might hold a French horn, or a very large viola, even though this did not agree with his camouflaged collared shirt or black boots. Still, I assumed he was a musician, until he began his speech:

"Hello, everyone. I'm here to show you my most prized possession, something that is very near and dear to my heart and part of my identity as a person." At this point, he unlatches the case and pulls out a hunting bow, followed closely by a hunting arrow. Now, the year was 1981, way before "weapons" (including toy weapons) were banned from school. At this time, you could bring these kinds of things to school as long as it was for educational purposes. No one believed he would be roaming the halls ready to discharge an arrow through the heart of the student who had been bullying him or the vice principal who had suspended him unfairly. It was perfectly acceptable, and no one had questioned his intentions upon entering the school that morning.

If you have never seen a hunting bow up close, it's quite an amazing apparatus. It's basically a high-tech machine, made out of aluminum, or some kind of shiny metal, and looks like something someone needed to program or use as a shield against attack. It was certainly nothing like the bow you'd see on those old Westerns, which looked clumsy and rubbery. And the arrow Jordan produced was unnerving as hell. The arrow head consisted of a series of razor blades arranged in a triangular fashion to maximize penetration. I was afraid to touch it for fear of nicking my finger and drawing blood.

To me (a person uninformed and ignorant of hunting culture), the whole unfolding scenario alerted and challenged my common sense. I had a compelling urge to tell Jordan to stop, to put away his instruments of danger, and to not worry about his grade. Under the circumstances, I'd compensate him handsomely for his efforts thus far. But that would have appeared rude and cowardly, so instead, I anxiously awaited his next move as he continued to enthusiastically address the class:

"As you can see, everyone, this is my hunting bow and arrow. I've had many fun times hunting with these, and I'll tell you about that in a minute. But right now, I'd like to show you how it works." At this juncture, he picks up the bow and continues:

"Here's how you hold it for maximum accuracy. It weighs about six pounds, and you must keep your body positioned like this. Notice how the bow string is very taut, and it takes more strength than you think to pull it back, aim, and hit your target. Let me demonstrate." At this point, he's holding the bow with his left hand and picks up the arrow with his right.

"Now, you must place the arrow in the bow properly, like this. Then relax, bend your elbow, and use two fingers to pull the string back until the bowstring is at full draw."

He's actually poised to fire the arrow! And it appears to be aimed directly at *me*! My instincts are telling me to duck immediately, but my fear froze me, thus preventing me from doing it. I now know how a bull's-eye feels prior to being pierced. In my mind, there was a good chance Mr. Wong would no longer exist if Jordan's fingers happened to slip, and let go of the bowstring, thus allowing the arrow to traverse the room and penetrate my chest. I halfheartedly had a near-death experience, remembering odd things from my childhood and having dreamlike visions of the peace and contentment of heaven. I also wondered what the newspaper article would say about this most unusual school incident the next day:

Teacher Killed by Arrow

A high school language arts teacher was killed yesterday after a hunting arrow had pierced his chest. Students immediately called the nurse, but she arrived too late to save Mr. Wong from bleeding to death. Apparently, the incident occurred during a speech on bow hunting by a student. Mr.

Wong had required all students to give a speech on their most important possession. The validity and wisdom of such an assignment will be thoroughly investigated by the superintendent and school board to determine if future policies need to be put into place to prevent future tragedies.

Just as these nauseating thoughts were coursing through my grisly imagination, and as I was waiting for the inevitable slip of Jordan's fingers, he relaxed the bow string and removed the arrow. Though somewhat agnostic in philosophy, I found myself instantaneously religious. Thank you, Lord! I promise to embrace all Ten Commandments close to my bosom. And please, God, strike me down if I do not forever uphold all your most devout moral standards. Thank you for letting me live!

The rest of Jordan's speech had no meaning to me. It was a blur. I was in such a satisfied state of relief that I could barely concentrate on what he was saying. It barely mattered anyway. I was alive and had a healthy, productive life ahead of me! I would be able to go home and hug my wife and two dogs. My perspective on life had been altered. Those stupid inconveniences most people fret about barely touched my psyche. The phrase "Don't sweat the little things" took on a revitalized relevance. My new definition of *happiness* pretty much included all human experiences, except death. I think you get what I'm trying to convey here.

Needless to say, Jordan received an A+ on his speech. He was quite pleased. I did mention to him, however, that drawing the arrow in a position to fire it was probably not safe. He laughed heartily and assured me there was nothing dangerous about it at all. He had been hunting with a bow and arrow since he was ten and, for all practical purposes, was an expert.

The next year, when it was time to do the required speeches, I changed the whole criteria. We would be spending two days in the library to research an author of their choice. Then students would prepare a speech on that author. One very important consideration was that no props or visual aids of any kind were allowed. If any student happened to forget this, the highest grade they could receive would be a D.

The speeches ended up being unbearably boring. I didn't even bother to wake up the three students who were sleeping, or the seven others who were writing notes, filing their nails, or staring at the clock. It took all of my energy to attend to the speeches myself. As I wrote comments on each student's talk, I noticed they began to take on a generic appearance. My mind wandered to that delicious leftover lasagna I brought for lunch. Then, for some odd reason, that made me think about the diapers I needed to pick up at the store for my one-year-old daughter. Yes, the whole day was extremely long and physically painful.

Yet I had the fortitude to plow through the speeches that day with great pleasure. I was absolutely thrilled that these speeches were free from the chance of being accidentally killed.

Chapter 5

Urination Education— Part 1

I read something the other day that made me urinate all over myself. It was a sign that said "Toilets Closed."

One major irritant about teaching is that your daily schedule is very rigid and uncompromising. When that nasty bell rings, you have before you thirty students waiting for your direction. *You* are ultimately responsible for these youngsters, and you alone.

Unfortunately, if you need to go to the bathroom really badly, you are taking a chance leaving these kids to their own determined resolve, even for a minute. I can remember many times racewalking (running in the hallway is against school rules) to the restroom, trying to urinate as fast as I possibly could. I'd push and squeeze it out with much haste, hoping to save a few precious seconds. It's funny how, when you are in a hurry, it seems like the time it takes to pee lasts forever even though it's less than twelve seconds, not counting the two or three shakes at the end. Anyway, while this necessary tinkling is occurring, my mind is brimming over with worrisome questions. Are the students throwing pencils and erasers at each other? Is Bobby, the class clown, mimicking me in front of the class? Is the two dollars' worth of change still in my desk? Did a student jump out the window, thinking his absence would not be noticed? I hurriedly zip up my pants and racewalk back to class and, in an effort to save a few seconds, skip washing my hands.

So trying to get anything done, other than teaching, during class time is nearly impossible. I guess there is "passing time" where you may be able to squeeze something in (or out). Passing time refers to that five minutes between classes that is given to students in order to move from one class to the next. At the last school I taught at, they lowered the passing time to four minutes. The administrators felt five minutes was too much time and, in fact, *caused* students to be tardy to class. The logic was that students had too much time so they would stop and talk to their friends, thus lose track of time, causing them to be tardy. Off hand, this sounds sort of ridiculous, but in middle school, it actually made a lot of sense. The problem was that it shaved off another minute a teacher could have used between classes to…well, urinate or something.

To make this even worse, I recall one year when the principal *required* all teachers to be in the hallway during passing times. The school was experiencing some problems during this time, like students pushing each other, yelling at each other, throwing things, making out (or worse), and swearing. You know, the normal kind of stuff. But sometimes fights would break out. So stationing teachers in the hallways was one proven way to lower the chance of these kinds of incidences occurring. Although having teachers in the hallways made sense, it did little for giving teachers time to get their personal tasks done. And it caused another problem. While I'm standing in the hallway, students are entering my classroom unsupervised. Who's watching my classroom? No one! So here I am standing in the hallway while destructive student shenanigans may be happening inside my classroom. My mind is racing. I might as well have been peeing in the bathroom.

So as you can see, there's virtually no time for the teacher to take care of normal personal responsibilities or obligations during the school day. If you are reading this and *not* a teacher, you know that this does not apply to you. If you're an office worker, you can go to the bathroom without unfavorable scenarios running through your head. And you probably have time to wash your hands. If you are a construction worker, you can probably let your foreman know you are making a quick twenty-minute trip to the bank, and nothing bad will happen. If you are working at a fast food restaurant, a quick "Hey, Donny, cover for me while I do my thing" will usually suffice.

It would be nice if teachers had somebody to "cover for them" while they "did their thing," but alas, there is no one. The only possibility is the principal or vice principal, and most teachers would not dream of asking them. It is just not the normal modus operandi in public education to ask the principal to cover for you while you go to the bank. And quite frankly, even if the principal offered to cover for you, nothing constructive would get done in class anyway. This is not necessarily the principal's fault, though. It's just that teaching is complicated and content driven. A teacher would not logically expect the average principal to explain the causes of World War I, the parts and functions of cells, or the mathematical theorem pertaining to solving the problem at hand, or teach *anything* specific that goes on in the average classroom at any given minute. The teacher needs to be there. The principal would just be babysitting. And if the principal actually attempted to teach, the damage done might take days to repair.

Now, there is always lunchtime to get things done, right? Wrong! The maximum amount of time a teacher gets for lunch is thirty minutes. It takes five minutes to get to and from the staff lounge and another five to get your lunch out, prepare it, and greet your colleagues. So realistically, you have twenty minutes. Furthermore, I know many, many teachers who (because of the high demands of teaching) work through their lunch period. As they are eating their sandwich, they are writing lesson plans, cutting out gold stars, or grading papers. If you are a parent, I'm sure you have noticed some smudges on your daughter's school papers. Your daughter has no idea how they got there, while you are lecturing her on the importance of keeping her assignments neat and clean. Well, it's not her fault! That smudge is mayonnaise from the teacher's sandwich or grease from the chicken your daughter's teacher was trying to cram down her throat during her diminutive eating time. If it's a rather sizable brown smudge, it's coffee, I assume. If it's a yellow smudge, it's mustard, lime Gatorade, or cream corn. Beets can cause some really disgusting reddish purple smudges. And if the spot is of dubious origin with a rather ambiguous color to it, it's probably leftover tuna casserole.

Needless to say, teachers must get their errands done outside of the school day. This is why the following incident posed such a predicament for me. I was teaching high school in the early 1980s. During this period of time, male teachers were expected to wear slacks and a collared shirt, at least. A tie and dress shoes were what most male teachers commonly added to their wardrobe. I was a casual kind of guy, so I opted for the slacks and collared shirt only.

At this time, I was six feet and about 260 pounds. I was a little on the chubby side, but my excuse was that I was playing semipro football as an offensive lineman and needed to keep my weight up. (I have *no* excuse now.) So with my rather generous size and the fact that tight slacks were the "in" style, it was only a matter of time before something interesting would happen.

One beautiful day in April, my students were working silently on an assignment at their desks. As the saying goes, you could literally hear a pin drop. I was sitting at my desk when I noticed a piece of paper lying on the floor about ten feet from me and located in front of the class. Curiosity getting the best of me, I got up, shuffled over to the paper, and bent over.

Rrrrriiiiiiipppp!

And when I say *rip*, I mean in the loudest possible outcry of fabric severing possible. The class next door surely heard it and was disrupted.

The teacher next door, unsure of the exact cause of the errant burst of noise, began reassuring her students that it was nothing and that they should continue with the lesson at hand.

Meanwhile, in my classroom, I initially smiled and even gloated at the obviously humorous happening that just took place. As I picked up the piece of paper just after the boom of my pants splitting apart, I fully expected an uncontrollable burst of laughter coming from the students. But a most unusual thing occurred. Instead, students were dead quiet with their eyes diverted to their books. Had they failed to hear the blast of thunder that caused commotion in the room next door but nary affected the students in the classroom where the noise had originated? I couldn't believe it. I was mystified to say the least. I was even ready for a clever response, such as, "Yes, class, they don't make slacks like they used to!" or "I hope I didn't wake up the principal!" or "It sucks to be fat!" But no student was acting as if they heard the loud rip at all!

With the most composed voice I could muster, I addressed the class:

"Class, let me have your attention, please. I have just ripped my pants. [I grabbed the manila folder on my desk.] I need to go to the office, get permission to go home, and get another pair of pants. I will be back shortly."

As I approached the door, I carefully shifted the manila folder to cover my behind. Still confused at the student's most tranquil reaction, I closed the door behind me and began to clandestinely make my way to the office. At the exact moment the door closed, a roar of uncontrollable laughter permeated the thick classroom door. I began to laugh myself at the absurd situation that had just unfolded.

Upon reflection, and as I was making my way to the office, I felt that the refrain of initial laughter from the students was so refreshing and wonderful. The students were so embarrassed for me that they pretended not to hear the obvious offensive sound of my pants ripping. I found this unbelievable and extremely mature of them.

As I departed for home to get another pair of pants, the normally imagined classroom chaos was pleasantly absent from my mind. I *knew* that I could trust these students. I threw on another pair of pants and even took some time to urinate and returned to school with clean hands as well.

Chapter 6

Urination Education—
Part 2

Three boys were having a peeing contest on a wall, trying to aim as high as possible. But one of the mothers happened by and scolded them for making a mess on a public wall. When the fathers asked their sons about what the mother did to them, the sons said, "She hit the roof!" The fathers then replied, "Did she win?"

I taught with a wonderful staff during a sixteen-year period at a middle school. They were dedicated, intelligent for the most part, and ready for some fun outside of school. Our staff used to go out almost every Friday after school to the local watering hole. Our principal was a willing participant in these outings, and this is why there were large crowds at these gatherings. On many occasions, up to twenty-five teachers would show up. After all, if your leader is coming, there must be something good about it. Maybe some teachers felt it was a great way to suck up to the boss. Whatever the case may be, these "meetings at the office," as we secretly called them, brought the staff together and made for a tight faculty who would go the extra mile for each other. As a result, we developed lifelong friendships and cared for each other, which carried over to the school setting.

Anyway, there was this particular male teacher whom I will call Gary. Gary was quite an amazing guy with many fascinating stories to tell. He had been a dog handler during the Vietnam War and, although no one actually saw it, said he had his picture on the front of *Time* magazine in the 1960s. He wore a neatly cropped mustache, and the wrinkles around his eyes when he smiled were a permanent fixture. He talked at a hurried pace, as if he knew he wouldn't have enough time to finish his tale. And he laughed vigorously after every few sentences, whether there was something funny or not. When I first met him, he was in his fifties, but he was as hip, energetic, and vibrant as your average twenty-five-year-old.

So one Friday night at the bar, the conversation came up about peeing in public restrooms. This is the kind of topic that generally surfaces when there are a bunch of guys around. One of the teachers began bragging about how he could step back six feet from the urinal, pee, and not lose a drop to the floor.

Gary then interrupted and announced how he has stepped all the way back to the wall of the restroom (a good twelve feet!), urinated, and not lost one drop to the floor. And with liquid courage coursing through his veins, he boldly broadcasted that he could "pee completely over a van without a drop touching the van proper."

Now, if you are female and reading this, you are probably already sickened and disgusted. But you have to realize that this is the kind of stuff guys love, especially if they have been indulging a bit. So bets were subsequently sequestered, arranged, and bantered about throughout the following school week. The proof of such a magnificent endeavor would take place the next Friday at our usual watering hole, over the 1992 red Plymouth Chrysler van, owned by none other than me.

There was much anticipation during the week over the outcome of this bet. Gary, of course, was presenting himself with nothing but the utmost confidence, while his male teacher friends were appropriately harassing him, kidding him, and expressing their doubt in his abilities to accomplish this amazing liquid performance. And this is what all really good male friends do. Guys cutting down other guy friends is part of the proper guy code of conduct.

The fateful Friday finally arrived, and naturally, Gary wanted to consume several beers to prepare his body, and his urethra, for the dirty deed. After his third beer, Gary proclaimed his readiness, and a small group made their way to the parking lot outside where my van was peacefully resting. The eager onlookers positioned themselves in front of the van so as to better determine if any drop did, in fact, brush the van.

The moment of truth arrived. Gary whipped it out and began to relieve himself. Amazingly, the stream easily poured over the top of my van and landed in an unsuspecting spot clear of the vehicle! But as this was happening, the observers, and myself, began to laugh uncontrollably. This was clearly one of the most humorous spectacles we have ever witnessed.

Gary heard us laughing and began to laugh himself at the absurd situation at hand (literally). As a result, his right hand, which was controlling his golden surge, jerked and caused his river of shame to change course. It, in fact, struck my van with such force the watery substance ricocheted upward and a geyser of yellow liquid drenched my van. This man clearly had to relieve himself!

We all, including myself, roared at this turn of events and, as all good guy friends will do, turned immediately to the validity of Gary's claim. Some pee had definitely cleared the van, but some had not, so did he really win the bet? This is the kind of crap guys live for.

A few minutes later, we were back inside where high-fives were freely bestowed amongst Gary and the lucky group of witnesses. Yes, female readers, there is no reason in hell for any celebrating to be going on at all. What had just happened was pretty ridiculous and technically illegal. But guys need to legitimize some of the stupid stuff they do.

I was still giggling as I got in my van to go home. And I can recall with great lucidity the sticky door handle and the rather salty fragrance that had infiltrated the confined atmosphere of my van.

My wife was wondering why I was washing our van the next day since it looked completely clean. I think I told her something about how I noticed a dog lifting its leg on the side of the van when coming out of the bar the night before.

Chapter 7

Mikayla: Model Student

If there were no schools to take children away from the home (part of the time), the insane asylums would be filled with mothers.

—Edgar W. Howe

After thirty-four years of teaching, I've estimated I have had over four thousand students in my classrooms, ranging in age from twelve to eighteen. With this many students over the years, I have seen every kind of personality and classroom behavior known to mankind. Truthfully, though, the vast majority of my students have been cooperative and at least somewhat motivated. On the other hand, I've had students who sat in class and did absolutely nothing all year. And these students were usually shocked when they failed the class! Also, I've had students who worked so hard I wondered about their health and welfare.

For example, I was teaching a novel called *Skid Road* to my ninth grade students in my Pacific Northwest history class. The students were issued the books so they could take them home if they wanted or needed to. When they returned the books to me after the unit, I noticed something strange about a book I got back from a girl from Vietnam who had been in the country a couple of years at most. There appeared to be these scratches in pencil above all the words in this two-hundred-page novel. Upon closer inspection, I realized she had translated every single word in the book into Vietnamese and wrote it very small above the words in the book! This must have taken her at least a couple of hours every night. And this was her homework in only *one* of her five classes. As the old joke goes, when you look up the word *persevere* in the dictionary, you'll see her picture.

I've also had my share of gangbangers, knuckleheads, sociopaths, weirdos, and criminals. Most of the bad behaviors exhibited by students, however, are a result of problems at home. Some students have terrible situations they must deal with, such as parental divorce, drugs in the home, physical and mental abuse, neglect, alcoholism issues, financial problems, or medical problems with themselves or with family members. I can remember one unfortunate eighth-grader who was very concerned about doing well in school but failed the class because she was constantly absent. I found out that she was the sole caretaker of her wheelchair-bound mother who was dying of cancer. It is a wonder how students with these kinds of problems are able to function at all in school. But one of these students, out of all the others, stick out in my memory. I'll call her Mikayla.

Mikayla came to my eighth grade language arts class midyear. Upon first impression, she was a model student. She was very attentive, asked a lot of good questions, and wanted to know about extra credit or about any way she could get her desired grade of A. In fact, she seemed to go a little overboard in her enthusiasm to succeed. Nevertheless, it was rather refreshing from my point of view to have such a motivated new student.

Physically, Mikayla was a little on the heavy side and wore thick, slightly out-of-date glasses. She carried herself with confidence, though, and seemed to have the maturity of a much older person. She talked freely with the other students, almost as if she had known them for a while. There was this toughness about her mannerisms also. And it seemed like she was trying too hard to make friends.

Anyway, one day, about three weeks after her arrival, I had finished my lesson with about three minutes left in the period. Rather than make up something extra for the students to do, which would have been easily recognized by the students and not appreciated, I decided to give them the last three minutes to wind down and get ready to leave for their next class. The students deserved a little free time, anyway. Their participation in the lesson was exemplary, and I felt they deserved it. Unfortunately, this ended up being a big mistake on my part.

The students began congregating near the door, which is normal. The idea is they can leave quickly and enjoy their four minutes of passing time. A few remained at their desks, but there were about twenty students clustered close together waiting to depart. Meanwhile, I'm at my desk, keeping a watchful eye when I heard a student (I will call Gill) say something to Mikayla:

"Hey, Mikayla, those glasses you are wearing are super cool!" Now, Gill was one of those fourteen-year-olds who believed he should be able to do anything he wants to in class. He can talk anytime to anyone for any reason. He could not fathom why I might call on him to stop. From his point of view, I was putting a major crimp in his social style. As a result, I had many exchanges with Gill like this:

"Excuse me, Gill, please stop talking while I'm trying to explain this assignment."

Completely caught off guard and totally perplexed, Gill responds by saying, "What? What did I do? I was just asking Connor about lunch today."

"Exactly," I respond with a matter-of-fact tone of voice, "that's what I'm trying to tell you. You are talking and missing the important instructions and causing Connor to miss them too. And I'd prefer *not* to repeat these instructions later just for you two."

"I can't believe how unfair you are, Mr. Wong," Gill counters with a perturbed look. "We, can't even do anything in this class."

Yes, Gill was what teachers so affectionately refer to as a big jerk. The world revolved around him, and he fed off the negative attention he received. He was a troublemaker and enjoyed stirring things up. So his question about Mikayla's glasses was not legitimate. It was completely ironic and mean. And his sly smirk as he asked it was more than obvious.

Mikayla, having the maturity of an adult, recognized this immediately and clearly did not appreciate it. She stiffened slightly and asserted to Gill:

"Gill, I don't appreciate your comment."

"But I was just trying to be nice to you," Gill replied with the same sickening smirk he had before. "I've never seen glasses so thick." With this, two of Gill's similarly immature friends began giggling.

Just then, Mikayla's entire demeanor began to change. Her body became rigid, she clenched her fists, and her maddened eyes targeted Gill's disrespectful remarks:

"Gill, you better shut up, and you better shut up *now*!"

"But, Mikayla," Gill continued, "I'm just trying to compliment you. Those glasses are so fashionable."

Mikayla was now ready to explode. "Shut up, Gill, *shut up*!"

I jumped up from my desk as Mikayla was stepping toward the still-smiling Gill. In as calm a voice as I could muster, I tried to defuse the situation, "Mikayla, please calm down. Come over here for a minute and ignore Gill."

Unfortunately, Mikayla was too wound up. Gill had pushed her buttons. She was inconsolable and ready to lash out at anyone in her way, which happened to be me at that moment.

"Fuck you, Mr. Wong, fuck you, you fat fuck!"

Okay, this was my first experience with a student telling me to fuck off.

But what really hurt was the *fat* adjective she used in front of fuck. I admit, I was a bit overweight, but I did lift weights every once in a while, and some portion of me was muscle. Nevertheless, teachers must be professional in these circumstances and not lower themselves to the fledgling, out-of-line comments of a fourteen-year-old. So to this end, I whispered to Mikayla that she needs to follow me to the office. After a few choice, unmentionable phrases directed at Gill, she actually followed me to the door. As I closed the classroom door, I noticed Gill was still smirking. He had successfully accomplished his goal.

On the way to the office, I tried to pacify Mikayla's enraged state of mind, but alas, that was impossible, as I soon found out:

"Mikayla, it's okay. I saw how Gill was egging you on. But you need to tell me, and I'll handle Gill for you. And you cannot swear in class."

Mikayla did not buy a word of it and, again, blurted out, "Fuck you, Mr. Wong. Fuck you, you fat fuck."

Ouch! There's that *fat* word again, for a second time! I obviously realized I could not say or do anything to rectify Mikayla's elevated mood. So the rest of the walk to the vice principal's office was done in silence. I explained to the VP what had happened and returned to class, leaving Mikayla in the VP's trusty hands.

I never saw Mikayla back in class again. The VP had suspended her, and she never returned to school. After all of this had happened, the school counselor explained to me that Mikayla was living a pretty tough existence. Her dad was absent. Her mom was a crack addict. And she was the sole caretaker of her two younger siblings. As a fourteen-year-old, she had experiences most of us will never have to deal with. Given her "model student" persona upon first arriving in my class, I never would have guessed the abominable conditions she was living under. It was truly a sad situation.

About seven years later, I was in line at Sam's Club. I gave the checkout clerk at the cash register my club card, per Sam's Club policy. She looked at it, paused a moment, and then remarked, "Are you Mr. Wong who taught language arts when I was in eighth grade?"

Not initially recognizing who she was, I replied, "Yes, that's me."

"I'm Mikayla, I was in your class seven years ago for a couple of weeks. Do you remember me?"

"Yes, Mikayla, I remember you very well."

"Well, Mr. Wong, I was going through a bunch of bad stuff at that time. But I have my life together now. I'm married and have a little daughter at home, and things are going great."

"That's wonderful, Mikayla. I'm so happy for you."

I really wanted to ask her if she still thought I was fat, but I thought the better of it. And as the old joke goes, if you look up the word *resilient* in the dictionary, you'll see Mikayla's picture.

Chapter 8

The Battle of the Bulge

You could be the ripest, juiciest peach in the world, and there's still going to be somebody who hates peaches.

During World War II, there occurred a battle in Nazi-held Belgium from December 16, 1944 through January 16, 1945. The Allied troops engaged the Germans, who ended up becoming unsuccessful in their attempt to push the Allies back from German home territory. This battle was one of the many important turning points in World War II and signaled the end of German domination in Western Europe. This battle was called the Battle of the Bulge, and the word *bulge* referred to the wedge that the Germans had previously driven into the Allied lines.

I'm sure, by now, I've totally sparked your historical interest. In my experience as a social studies teacher, it seemed that history was everyone's favorite subject (...not!). Thus, I know you are eager to read more about the Battle of the Bulge and its effects on the outcome of World War II. As I mentioned earlier, it is crucial we all know our past and how it defines us today.

The Battle of the Bulge, however, has two meanings for me. As I have already said, the word *bulge* referred to the wedge the Germans had carved into Allied-held European territory. But when I think of the word *bulge*, another, more personal, scenario comes to mind. *Bulge* can also refer to the lump protruding from the front crotch area of a man's pants. You know, that protrusion that so innocently forms between a guy's Netherlands and whatever he is wearing. The tighter the slacks, sweats, jeans, or swimsuit, the more pronounced the bulge could be. Very loose fitting pants may totally hide any expectant bulge. Unfortunately, almost every day of teaching middle school, I wore sweatpants or sport pants, which, evidently, do little for bulge-hiding. And I discovered this was apparently a problem one year while teaching language arts to eighth-graders.

As a teacher of thirty-four years, I learned that, no matter what you do or don't do, you will always have some students who hate your guts. You could be the most gifted, interesting instructor in the universe, but inevitably, there will be at least one kid who despises you. After a few years, I pretty much gave up finding out why a particular student hated me—because it usually made no difference in terms of changing the student's outlook. Besides, sometimes what the student hated about you was something you could do little or nothing about. They may dislike you because of the way you look. Maybe you remind him of his mean uncle or neglectful father. It could be what you wear, the tone of your voice, or the way you walk. You can't change these things very easily, or at all.

At the same time, there will always be at least one student who loves you, and again, you might not know the reason for it. You hope it's because of your riveting lectures, stimulating lesson plans, or fun classroom activities. Maybe it's that you challenged them academically and they learned a lot.

But it probably isn't. They may like you for what you *don't* do. For example, I've had many students tell me they really appreciate the fact that, in eighth grade language arts, I do not require them to give speeches in front of the class. I guess there are a high percentage of kids who are deathly afraid of the possibility of embarrassing themselves in front of their somewhat unkind and unforgiving peers. Thus, I was their favorite teacher. In addition, I asked my thirteen-year-old daughter, who was a straight A student, who her favorite teacher was, and she responded immediately with her science teacher. When I asked why, she said because she dresses really cool. So I stopped worrying a long time ago about whether a student likes or dislikes me. The only thing I could do was be myself and perform my teaching duties as best I could.

One year while teaching eighth grade language arts, I had a student I will call Chloe. From the first day of class, it was clear that Chloe loathed me. She often sat in her desk, facing away from me, when I was addressing the class. When I asked her to please turn around, she sneered, mumbled a distasteful phrase about me under her breath, and minutely moved her neck so that her peripheral vision barely made contact with the half of my body that was facing her. She rarely did any work in class. And if I approached her to try to get her going, she'd stiffen, glare, and actually make several thrusting movements toward me, as if to warn me to come no closer, or she would do me some serious bodily harm. I noticed she seemed quite amiable when talking with other students, though. But with me, her demeanor was pervading with hate, disgust, and with an abhorrence only seen by a mother toward the murderer of her only child. I honestly could not figure out why she disliked me. And I learned *not* to approach her to find out.

Unknown to me, Chloe had been making frequent visits to the school counselor to try to transfer out of my class. The school counselors were responsible for student schedules, but it was rare for students to transfer to another teacher after the school year began. I averaged maybe *one* student every year who transferred, either out or into my class after the school year started. Counselors did not like students to transfer. There had to be a very, very, very compelling reason if it occurred. The reason would have to be of an emergency nature. For example, I had one student who, whenever she came into my classroom, began coughing and became sick. She wasn't faking, and we couldn't figure out what environmental factors were present in my room causing this. In fact, she expressed an avid interest in staying in my class. However, when she was in the other language arts teacher's room, she was fine. So they ended up transferring her due to health reasons. During my career, I have had maybe three students come into my class due to emergency reasons and maybe two students leave. So as you can see, the reason for transferring to another teacher must be big, really big. I soon found out how big Chloe's reason was for getting out of my class, on one fine day in October, about six weeks after the school year started.

I happened to be in the main office, checking my mailbox that afternoon, just after the bell rang to dismiss students for the day. There were a few other teachers present. I was chatting with one of them when I saw the principal approaching me.

"Hello, Mr. Wong, may I speak with you in my office for a moment?"

The principal, I'll call him Mr. Highland, was in his second year at the school. He had spent most of his career as a vice principal at the nearby high school. He came here for his last two years in public education before retiring. Everyone knew the reason was to pad his pension, even though he denied it to the staff. Anyway, he was a nice enough guy but was rather aloof. He wore his glasses about a quarter way down his nose, so his eyes were hiding behind his frames, and his bushy mustache concealed his mouth. His attire advertised his generic conservatism. You know, white collared shirt, dark single-colored tie, and dark blue or black slacks. When he spoke, it was in a monotone voice complimented by an expressionless face. He could have easily passed (personality-wise) as Mr. Spock's brother on Star Trek, minus the pointed ears of course. As a result, no one really knew where he was coming from or how he was feeling, whether he was serious or joking. Words alone, without the accompanying body language, oral intonations, and facial expressions leave the receiver of the information baffled. So I knew I may have to do some acute interpretations, depending on what he was about to tell me.

Also, being called into the principal's office for a private chat is usually not a good thing. It's *never* a good thing if you are a student, and almost never a good thing if you are a teacher. So with foreboding feelings permeating my thoughts, I made my way into Mr. Highland's office and closed the door behind me.

"Mr. Wong, you currently have a student in your second period class named Chloe Jackson," Mr. Highland mundanely began.

"Yes, that's correct," I responded, not sure if what he said was a question or a statement of fact.

"Well, we'll be moving her from your class to Mrs. Trable's class beginning Monday. The counselor has made the arrangements."

I hesitated a few moments and then continued, "I'm just curious, Mr. Highland, if you don't mind, may I know the reason for the transfer?"

Mr. Highland stared at me, emotionless, and I heard these words come out of his mouth:

"Well, Mr. Wong, she said she was repulsed and disgusted when you stand in front of the class, or sit on your desk, while addressing the class. Quite frankly, she's grossed out by seeing your bulge."

Now initially, I thought it was a joke and almost began laughing. But Mr. Highland was not the kind of guy who joked around. So I looked at him to try to get some sort of "reading" from him, which, as I explained earlier, was impossible.

Without thinking, I looked Mr. Highland in the eyes, tilted my head, and looked at my so-called bulge and looked back at him just before uttering this statement of fact.

"Mr. Highland, what would you like me to do about it?"

Many things were running through my mind at this juncture. My response was supposed to be at least halfway funny. After all, I am a grown man, and I'm going to have a bulge of some sort, and there's nothing I can do about it, short of a painful operation and reassignment to the opposite sex. But it was also meant to be a serious defensive statement. Since I apparently have a noticeable bulge, does this mean I can only teach boys? And wouldn't some boys be disgusted as well? Once word got around that all you had to do to get out of Mr. Wong's class was tell the counselor you had nightmares about Mr. Wong's bulge, then my class size may be drastically decimated, if you get my meaning. I can just see the line at the counselor's office and the counselor peeking her head out of her door telling the students to take a number and be respectfully courteous and patient while waiting. And if students were repulsed, then staff members may be as well. When I get my morning coffee in the staff lounge, will staff members get up and leave, cupping their hands around their mouths? How can I possibly walk down the hallway without a myriad of students convulsing in agony? Dare I step into the lunchroom without students covering their eyes for fear of stomach cramps and upchucking? Will the staff, and students alike, circulate a petition demanding my resignation? This whole bulge thing could easily get out of hand and cost me my job!

Mr. Highland didn't see any humor, or seriousness, or anything of any consequence in my statement. He said nothing. Instead, he ever so slightly flicked his head toward the door as an indicator that I was excused and needed to go now.

For many months following this incident, I became somewhat paranoid about my bulge. I found myself secretly checking my bulge in class to see how noticeable it might be. Is it showing too much? Should I somehow turn around with my back to the students when giving instructions? Will holding a book in front of it increase student learning? Are students in the front row particularly disgusted? Is that why, as I am speaking to the class, Diane, a straight A student, has her head down? I found myself turning my torso slightly when speaking to students one on one. And I avoided, at all costs, walking up and down the rows of desks to check student work. Good God! My bulge would literally be at eye level! So for a few months, I must say that my bulge became a definite detriment to my heretofore excellent teaching.

Then I learned the real reason for Chloe's transfer. Her closest, forever best friend was in the other class. Her main reason for going to school was to socialize, and she couldn't stand being separated from her dear friend. Once she was placed in Mrs. Trable's class, she manipulated her way into a seat next to her friend and became a very happy camper indeed. Chloe wasn't the brightest student, but she did know that the excuse of "I want to be in the same class as my best friend" wasn't going to fly as a legitimate reason to transfer her. As a fourteen-year-old, you have to give her credit for some awesome creativity and inventiveness when trying to get her way with the adults surrounding her.

Chapter 9

A Boy Named Heather

"If there are any idiots in the classroom, will they please stand up," said the sarcastic teacher. After a long silence, one freshman rose to his feet.

"Now, mister, why do you consider yourself an idiot?" inquired the teacher.

"Well, actually, I don't," said the student, "but I hate to see you standing up there all by yourself."

Most people who ponder their public school years agree that middle school sucked. These grades included sixth to eighth grade, where you were somewhere between twelve and fourteen years old. At this age, peer pressure is at its highest. You may recall something you did that was pretty ridiculous, just because you were trying to conform to the group's expectations. I can remember drinking alcohol in the bushes next to the school, trying to smoke a cigarette (and coughing my lungs out!), and talking down to some of the "nerds," all because I thought that was what I needed to do to stay in favor with my peers.

In middle school, you also became acutely aware of the opposite sex. You may recall in elementary school how you thought of the opposite sex as dirty, icky, and dumb. You wouldn't have dreamed of playing with someone of the opposite sex on the playground. But when you reach middle school, your hormones are gearing up, and the opposite sex becomes oddly attractive. Unfortunately, you, as a thirteen-year-old, have no idea how to behave around this mysterious creature, and many social blunders occur. Again, you may recall some of the stupid, embarrassing stuff you did, trying to impress that boy or girl you thought was so cute. I can remember a girl in seventh grade, whom I had a crush on. She, in her cute little voice, remarked within earshot of me how her favorite color was yellow. So first, I insisted my mom take me shopping that evening. The next day, I confidently showed up to school in a yellow T-shirt and yellow sweatpants. I looked like a bloated banana. She will surely instantly fall in love with me now! I can remember, with much disappointment, that she never even noticed her favorite color, let alone come running to me with open arms and an elated smile, like I halfheartedly hoped she would.

Another difficult problem in middle school is the fact that everyone's body is changing, and changing at different rates. I taught middle school for twenty-two total years, and I have had fourteen-year-old girls so well developed that they could easily pass for nineteen or twenty. In the same class, however, there would be girls who looked like they were still in third grade. And I have had boys who could grow a full beard at fourteen and some who won't be touching a razor for five or more years. Unfortunately, when I was in eighth grade, I was the latter. In those days, students were required to take physical education *and* shower afterward. Well, this was a mortifying time for me since I had zero pubic hair. It seemed like all the other guys had at least some hair down there, yet I looked like a newborn baby. Needless to say, the proper placement of my hands and towel, during shower time, was crucial to my survival.

With middle school bodies in various stages of development, and with clothing styles being quite eclectic, the boundary between male and female was sometimes blurred in middle school. Sometimes, the student's name was what saved you, as a teacher, from making a terrible social mistake in class. And this is why I was so perplexed by this one particular student I had in eighth grade. The name was Heather, but he clearly was a boy.

On the first day of class, calling roll carefully is very important. Not only do we need an accurate count for state-funding purposes, but it is the first chance the teacher gets to meet their students. So in eighth grade language arts class, I was calling the students' names, and the next one on the roster was "Heather." Heather respectfully raised her hand. I looked up to acknowledge her presence. But there was a problem. Heather was a boy! I was initially a bit confused and took a double take. Yep, he certainly was a boy! Then I became sad and empathetic. I wondered why a parent would be so mean as to name their son Heather. I thought that maybe they really wanted a girl, and this was their sick way of pretending they had one. I felt a lot of sympathy for Heather having to go through fourteen years with that name, undoubtedly having been ridiculed, teased, and bullied. I made a promise to myself that I was going to make sure no one in my class even *thought* about messing with Heather because of his name.

I was also concerned that Heather's family was struggling financially. Literally, *every* day, he wore the same clothes to school—a T-shirt, blue jeans, and tennis shoes. It was a testament to my class, however, that no matter how hard I looked, I could not see students treating him badly. In fact, he appeared to be rather popular. He mingled easily with both boys and girls and was a cooperative model student. So maybe, I thought, he just wore what was comfortable. In fact, when I was in high school, that was pretty much what I wore every day, and the reason was partly financial, but mostly for comfort. So I concluded that this must be the reason, not that his family was needy.

Anyway, throughout the year, Heather was a pleasure to have in class. The name Heather still bothered me a bit, though. It definitely was a girl's name. It would have been easier for me if his name was Pat, Chris, or Taylor, or some other name that could go either way. So I decided to ask the teacher next door to me about my dilemma since she also had Heather in class.

One day, at lunch, I approached Ms. Betty Nygard to see if she had the same feelings about Heather:

"Hey, Betty, I was wondering if I could ask you something?"

"Sure, Rog, shoot."

"You know, both of us have Heather Jones in class, and I was wondering what you thought about the name Heather."

With a rather strange, quizzical look on her face, Betty shrugged her shoulders and replied, "I sort of like the name Heather!"

Okay, it must just be *me*. Maybe, unbeknownst to me, *Heather* is one of those names like Pat or Chris or Taylor. I have been known to be very naive and uninformed before, so I guess I've been stressing for no reason. I felt much better about Heather from then on—well, at least until the very last week of school.

Nine months had passed, and it was the last week of school. Everyone (especially teachers) were looking forward to summer break. And during the last week, there were many end-of-the-year fun activities for the students. One of these involved students signing up for a specific activity they would enjoy participating in. There was a variety of activities to choose from. Some were boys-only activities, such as football, basketball, or weight lifting. Some were girls-only activities, such as softball, volleyball, or sewing. And some were activities that either sex could sign up for.

So the teachers were asked to sign the students up in their respective homeroom classes, and I had Heather in my homeroom class. We would then give the list to the administrator after school. I was pretty excited for the students and began the sign-up process on the appointed day.

"Carlos, could you please come up to my desk and tell me which activity you'd like to sign up for?"

"I'd like football!" Carlos excitedly divulged.

"Great, Carlos, I think Mr. Manson, the PE teacher, will be supervising that group, so it should be a lot of fun. Come on up, Judy, and give me your choice."

"I really don't know, but I guess I'll sign up for sewing. None of the other activities sound good to me."

"Okay, Judy, but keep your head up. I bet it's more fun than you think. Now, Heather, it's your turn. Come on up."

"Mr. Wong, I'd like to do girl's softball."

I looked at him, thinking he was joking, of course. He obviously wanted to dominate the play or maybe knew a girl who was signing up he had a crush on. Or maybe he was, for the first time, expressing his sense of humor. Whatever his ruse was, I smiled broadly and responded by saying, "Now, Heather, you *know* you cannot sign up for girl's softball."

Confused, and with utter faith permeating her words, Heather replied, "But why not, Mr. Wong?"

Thinking he was continuing his out-of-place humor, my voice carried a determined seriousness, "Heather, you cannot sign up for girl's softball because you are a *boy*."

Now it was Heather's turn to become earnest. A solemn, candid look crossed her face, and she took a step closer to my desk. With an unwavering voice, I heard her response.

"What? *I am a girl!* My name is *Heather!*"

Yes, Heather had been a girl all along, and it only took me nine months to discover this fact. I went through the whole year thinking of Heather as a boy. I will concede that I'm definitely the class idiot on this one.

I learned later, however, that many other teachers at the school initially mistook Heather for a boy as well but eventually found out the truth in a day, a week, or maybe a month at most. I must point out that, in addition to her aforementioned clothing, she also had very short cropped hair, never wore any makeup, and carried herself much more like a male. And as far as female development, there was none. I found out later that, in fact, Heather was quite a seasoned softball player and went on to lead her high school team to many victories. So, Heather, if you are reading this, I totally apologize for my preposterous, inconceivable error.

Anyway, as an experienced teacher, my response to her telling me she was actually a girl involved some quick thinking. I desperately needed to redirect and lie. "I knew that, Heather! I was just kidding around since it's the last week of school and everything. Of course, you can sign up for girl's softball, and I'm sure you'll have a great time!"

I tried not to let the fact that I was turning red show too much.

Chapter 10

Coaching Blues

If you make every game a life-and-death proposition, you're going to have problems. For one thing, you'll be dead a lot.

—Dean Smith, University of North Carolina basketball coach

'm not trying to brag, but I was always a pretty good athlete growing up. I started off playing Pee Wee baseball at age ten and played until I reached high school, where I switched over to track and field. I seemed to be able to jump a little better than the average guy, and I ended up specializing in the triple jump. As far as I know, I still hold my high school's triple jump record of forty-four feet and three inches.

I also started participating in tackle football at age ten and played this sport through my junior year of high school, until I suffered a shoulder injury boxing. It required surgery and prevented me from playing football my senior year. Later in life, though, I played six years of semipro football. I was in my late thirties, and I had started weight training, bulked up to 260 pounds, and secured a starting position at center.

But my first love was basketball. I played basketball endless hours at the local gymnasium starting at age eleven. I had a core group of basketball-loving friends, and we honed our skills until high school. As a result, our high school team took fourth place in the state tournament. This doesn't seem like a huge achievement, but it was the highest ranking my high school had ever achieved in basketball. And forty-four years later, the school still hasn't achieved a higher place in the state. This led to three seniors getting full-ride college basketball scholarships, and one of those seniors was me. I ended up playing only one year at college, however. Nevertheless, my extensive exposure to different sports impacted my career as a public school teacher, especially my first few years.

As I've mentioned previously, I started my career at a high school teaching freshmen language arts and social studies. At this particular high school, there was always a shortage of coaches. It was a medium-sized high school with around a thousand students in four classes (freshmen through senior), but it had many competitive sports, all needing coaches. So when I interviewed for the teaching position, the principal, having looked over my résumé filled with sport's experience, asked me if I would be willing to do some coaching. He didn't name any specific sports where a coach was needed, but rather just asked, in general, if I'd do some coaching if he hired me. I enthusiastically said, "*Yes!*" At the time, this fit perfectly with my lifelong love of sports. I felt that the best thing next to playing sports would be coaching sports. It would allow me to be around the thrill and self-fulfilling spirit that sports had afforded me my entire life. I was very excited about the opportunity to coach at the high school level, and it showed in my answer to the principal's inquiry.

I quickly found myself coaching many sports from boys basketball and football to girls softball and volleyball during my first few years. And I found out something about coaching that was unexpected: I didn't like it. I didn't like it at all. In fact, I can say I hated it. I discovered there's a big difference between playing a sport and coaching it. And I just couldn't get myself to enjoy it, no matter how hard I tried.

First, coaching at the high school level is very, very, very time consuming, and the pay is miserable. One year, I calculated my hourly wage for coaching freshmen football, and it worked out to less than $5.00 per hour. This was at a time when the minimum wage in the state was $7.50. Secondly, I mistakenly went into coaching thinking that all the athletes were like me at that age—motivated, loving the game, willing to work hard, and playing with 100 percent effort. Boy, was I naive! I found out that many of the athletes were playing for the wrong reasons. Maybe a father was forcing his son to play, or maybe they wanted the status and glory, but none of the hard work. Maybe they were doing it for the sole purpose of getting a Letterman's jacket or trying to impress a girl or their parents. Maybe they believed they were good at that sport but in reality, sucked. Maybe they did it because their friends were on the team, or their home life was so bad that they would rather stay after school for any reason, rather than going home. There was a myriad of reasons high school athletes participated in sports, and many of those reasons were problematic from the coach's perspective.

Furthermore, coaching at the high school level was way too serious for me. I always had *fun* playing sports, but as a coach, you had many serious responsibilities and life-and-death decisions to make. I've had many parents imply, or actually, say, in a straightforward manner that I have ruined their son's or daughter's life. They will question me as to why their son isn't getting any playing time. The inevitable truth is that their son's skill level sucks; he is terrible, clumsy, uncoordinated, and he would embarrass himself, and the school, if he played. But the parents who ask this question do not recognize this brutal truth. So you, as the coach, have to be politically correct, polite, and tactful. As a respected coach, you must spontaneously come up with an euphemistic reason, such as mentioning the practice he missed two weeks ago or his slightly lower effort at practice or the coach's belief that he doesn't understand the system as well as the starting players. But it probably won't matter. The parent will still believe you have ruined his chances of getting a college scholarship, and thus a college degree, and subsequently living a happy future life.

As a coach, you also have to cater to all those bothersome, but necessary, extras that come with coaching a high school sport. This includes fund-raising, which is really irritating since the sport never seems to have enough money to function. And getting the players to sell candy or wash cars on Saturday is not something they want to do. They'd rather scrub the gym floor with a toothbrush. Then there is the paperwork of issuing uniforms and practice gear. That part's not too bad; but try getting this stuff from the players at the end of the season, and you will find there's more paperwork in the form of fines, as well as tracking down players around the school, and harassing them about giving back the school's property. Then there is the occasional unreasonable suggestion, or two, from the administration. Sometimes they believe they know more about your players and sport than you do. And you may have to manage an assistant coach who is unmotivated and/or ignorant about the sport and was hired simply to fill the position.

Needless to say, after about six years of coaching sports, I had had enough. I really, really hated coaching and was looking for any viable excuse to quit, for good, forever. The forthcoming birth of my second daughter afforded me a plausible reason to end the insanity. I had it all thought out. I'd go to the principal in charge of athletics and explain that I'll be having a new addition to my family. I'm sure he'll smile and congratulate me. Then I'll discreetly explain about some of the issues surrounding my wife's work schedule, day care, and juggling two young kids. Then I'll kindly request a one-year reprieve from coaching, with the promise of coaching again the following year. (But my secret hope was that they may find a coach who actually likes it and wants to stay, thus relieving me of this future burden.) I honestly did not think my request was unreasonable. I had more than paid my coaching dues, and it was time someone else stepped up to the plate.

The principal in charge of athletics at my school was a former coach himself, very sports-oriented and knowledgeable, and believed *all* coaches simply *loved* to coach. I'll call him Mr. Sarver. He was the typical suit-and-tie wearing vice principal. Never did he have a hair out of place, a wrinkle in his slacks, or shoes without a shine. He was, however, totally into everything having to do with sports, a true fifty-year-old "jock."

Mr. Sarver probably had fond memories of his coaching days and enjoyed immensely his time with his players and fellow coaches. Maybe he had players who went on to successful college athletic careers or even professional careers. His pride in knowing he had a part in that was, I'm sure, exhilarating to him. Whatever the case may have been, he honestly thought the entire school's coaching staff was totally delighted with the entire process of coaching. He seriously could not fathom a coach who did not like it. I never knew the extent of Mr. Sarver's athletic obsessiveness until our head football coach left for a coaching position out of state. This meant Mr. Sarver had the privilege of hiring a new head football coach. Now, this was a very serious matter indeed. The first step was to post the position through the school district's sites, as stipulated by district policies. Waiting the appropriate amount of time, he carefully read, and re-read, all written applications, eventually narrowing it down to the top three. Then, he took two days off from his school duties so he could travel to the school where the prospective candidates were currently coaching. While there, he would thoroughly interview school authorities about the character of the coach, visit the neighborhood where the coach resided, and ask community leaders about the candidate's community involvement and moral values. All of this was followed up by an intense two- to three-hour personal interview. Then he would repair to his office back home, discuss his findings with pertinent school personnel, think deeply about each candidate, and finally make his gut-wrenching decision. Now, keep in mind that, at this time, the hiring process for a teacher involved looking through some résumés, narrowing it down to a few, and calling them in for a ten- to fifteen-minute interview before making a decision. Even as a sports lover, this discrepancy in hiring head coaches versus teachers was repulsive to me.

Anyway, unknown to Mr. Sarver, his prosports stance, as described above, helped me reach my goal of never having to coach again. It was toward the end of the school year when Mr. Sarver was busy reviewing his coaching positions and who would fill them for the following year. This would be the perfect time to see him. He'd have plenty of time to find my replacement. So one Friday, right after school was dismissed, I walked into his office, smiled, and asked if I may speak with him for a few minutes.

"Well, sure, Roger, come on in, and have a seat! Hey, that kid Johnny Pualani really had a great season, didn't he? He'll probably end up going to a division II college, though. I don't think he's quite ready for the big time."

Mr. Sarver shifted his eyes to the ceiling and put his finger to his chin. He was deep in thought, probably about how the coach could have made Johnny ready for a division *I* university. He then realized I was in his office and snapped out of it.

"Uh, Roger, so what's on your mind?"

"Well, Mr. Sarver, I'm not sure if you know this, but my wife is pregnant, and we're expecting our second child in a few months."

"Congratulations! That's wonderful news, Roger!"

"Yes, well, thanks. And you know, I've been doing a lot of coaching while I've been here."

"And you've been doing a great job. I really appreciate your dedication."

"Well, thanks again, Mr. Sarver. I know you have kids yourself, and I know you are aware of the time commitment coaching requires. So quite frankly, with the birth of my second child, and with my wife's crazy work schedule, and trying to get day care, and all of that, I was wondering if I might take next year off, as far as coaching is concerned, so I can spend more time with my family. I promise I will coach again the following year."

At these powerful, unsuspecting words, Mr. Sarver's entire demeanor transformed. Gone was his smile and jolly, positive gesticulations. Instead, his eyes sharpened and peered intently at me. His lips quivered ever so slightly, and his back straightened. He looked like a man whose wife had just told him she's leaving him for another guy.

He started to articulate something but stopped suddenly, only to let a little droplet of saliva eject itself a couple inches from his trembling lips. A vein appeared on his forehead and began throbbing in unison with his increased heartbeat. I was fully expecting him to explode, literally, when he firmly, and loudly, finally replied, "*Fine!* If you don't want to coach next year, then you will not be coaching the following year either, or the year after that. In fact, *you'll never coach at this school again!*"

Now, I was initially taken aback at the very scary and threatening manner in which Mr. Sarver delivered these words. But my brain was working overtime, processing it, and I quickly came to a wonderful conclusion. This man actually thought I loved coaching, and he believed no punishment he could give me would be worse than never having the opportunity to coach again. Unbelievable! Yet so delightfully well-timed! So I decided to play along with it and give him the satisfaction of truly punishing me.

"But, Mr. Sarver," I sheepishly responded, "can't I come back the following year and coach…at least one sport?"

Barely allowing me to finish my question, and with an evil, yet giddy glare, Mr. Sarver slammed down his authoritative hammer. "*Absolutely not!* If you can't coach next year, then you are done coaching at this school for good."

I'm not an actor, but at this juncture, I attempted to water my eyes. I bowed my head ever so slowly, and with the most pitiful voice I could muster, I uttered, "Okay, Mr. Sarver."

I shuffled pathetically out of his office, looking like a hungry puppy who was denied food from its master and beaten with a stick as well. I continued this sorrowful spectacle all the way to the parking lot. I opened my car door and slinked into the driver's seat, started my engine, and began driving away.

Then I screamed with immense joy and deafening volume, "Hallelujah!"

Chapter 11

Safety First

I failed my health and safety class test today. Apparently, when they ask you, In the event of a fire, what steps would you take? "Fucking large ones" is not the correct answer.

Every month, the teachers and staff were required to perform three safety drills in school. A day, at the end of the month, was chosen for this purpose. On this day, we practiced all the drills—which included fire, earthquake, and lockdown drills. It usually took about twenty delightful minutes to complete all of them.

The students were usually pretty indifferent about these drills. Sure, they were happy about the twenty-minute break from class work, but they believed the drills were sort of silly. They thought that if something actually happened, like a real fire, they wouldn't follow drill procedures anyway. If a dangerous hot fire was close to them, for example, there would be general panic, with students and teachers running in all directions. I mean, if you are in a movie theater, and all of a sudden, you turn around to a blazing fire in the seat behind you, I don't think you are going to "remain calm and make your way to the nearest exit, row by row." I think you'll be running for your life, bumping into old ladies, mowing down toddlers, and shrieking at the top of your lungs while your hands are wildly gesticulating above your head. Okay, everyone is different, but the "fight or flight" response not only applies to an antelope cornered by a lion but to humans as well. I doubt you're going to "fight" the fire with your diet Coke, Hershey bar, and popcorn. Your brain will be screaming at you to scurry the hell out of the theater.

Anyway, the fire drill was a monthly ritual. At our school, they always let the teachers know beforehand about when the drill would take place. This was strictly for our convenience so that we might adjust our lesson plans accordingly. Also, this gave special education teachers a head start with their students who were in wheelchairs or had other mobility issues. If there was real fire, though, I'm assuming these students would be last out of the building and thus most likely to be found ablaze.

After the first few months of school, the students pretty much knew exactly what to do if the fire alarm sounded. In my case, the students knew to exit the classroom door, turn left, go down a flight of stairs, exit the building, take two quick lefts, and walk stoically to a predesignated gathering location. Here, they would form a single-file line in front of me. My duties, prior to leaving the room, were to grab a roster of my students, turn off the lights, close the door (but for Christ sakes, don't lock it; the firemen might need to get in there!), and place either a green or red sign on the outside of my door. A green sign meant everything is cool, we're all safe, and we made it out okay. A red sign meant there's trouble in this room—like a student not accounted for or some other issue that I cannot, for the life of me, imagine. A student passed out in class? Bunsen burners left on? Some psycho student with a death wish refused to leave? Let's just say I never had an occasion to leave a red sign outside my door.

The worst part of the fire drill was the fire alarm. The alarm at my school was *extremely* loud. It was also very high pitched, a cross between fingernails on a chalkboard and a screaming injured cat. I'm guessing the persons responsible for this obnoxious, deafening, and horrid alarm blast believed that the most important element was that everyone must hear it. Well, they succeeded in spectacular fashion!

In fact, they succeeded to the point that for several hours afterward, we were still hearing it...or was that just some darn loud ringing in our ears? My most common question from students the rest of the day was, "What?" If not for plugging my ears with my fingers when exiting the building, I'd be pissed off about never having taught my students sign language. And by the way, that student roster I needed to grab on the way out was tucked under my right armpit, and under constant jeopardy of falling, which created a lot of anxiety for me. If the roster hit the ground, which ear will I sacrifice?

Another issue with fire drills was the weather. Our November through March drills were sometimes semiunbearable. These drills were required, and if it was raining, or thirty-two degrees outside— oh well! Remember how the teachers knew ahead of time about the drill? Well, some teachers would show up to class wearing a heavy coat and gloves, which was a pretty big hint to the students about what was going to take place that period. So as we are standing outside, the students are uncharacteristically expressing an urgent, desperate desire to get back to class and continue their education.

During my thirty-four years teaching, I only experienced one "real" fire, but it was rather lame. A student had started a fire in a metal classroom garbage can, and the smoke was enough to set off the alarm. When the alarm sounded, the whole school evacuated just like we were supposed to do. Meanwhile, within a few seconds, a teacher had turned over the garbage can and extinguished the fire.

The next delightful drill was in case of an earthquake. During this drill, we were all supposed to crouch under our desks so as not to be hit by falling ceilings. Per drill specifications, we crouched under our desks for sixty seconds, which is actually a very long time. I can sense you don't believe me. Okay, I'll prove it to you. Let's count to sixty. Ready, begin. One thousand one, one thousand two, one thousand three, one thousand four...one thousand sixty. See! It's a lengthy time to be under a desk. And teachers were not exempt from this exercise. Due to my age and size, there was no way my whole body would fit under my desk. I basically had to choose between my lower body and my upper body. I figured if the ceiling fell and began severing body parts, I could probably live without legs. But without a head, I'd certainly be defunct. So here I was, under my desk on my stomach with my legs sticking out. I could only see through the four-inch space granted to me by the bottom of my desk. And what I saw were the bottom parts of students crouching under their desks—their shoes, socks, and shins mostly. This was a somewhat bizarre perspective. These were things I almost never consciously noticed about my students. Hey, Billy has shoes just like mine! He must shop at Costco too. My God, those lime green socks Nicky has on are awful! Dang, why are Christina's ankles all puffed up? Anyway, after sixty seconds had elapsed, we could get out from under our desks and resume class.

During my teaching career, there actually was one major earthquake. It happened on February 28, 2001, at 10:54 AM. It was a Wednesday, and it was third period.

I was sitting on top of my desk, addressing the class, when I heard a low, rumbling sound. Then the earth under us began moving. Now, if you have never been in an earthquake, my description might appear strange. But the movement of the earth felt like a wave. It was as if we were standing in a tiny rowboat in the middle of the ocean.

As soon as I recognized it was an earthquake, I yelled, "UNDER YOUR DESKS!" And a truly amazing thing happened. All the students did so immediately, just like we had been practicing every month. I remember being pleased and wonderfully astounded at the same time. All those silly drills had actually worked!

The earthquake lasted forty-five seconds. That's not sixty, but still a lengthy time to wait for the ground underneath you to stop moving. Another interesting observation was that the students were noticeably different. Instead of the muffled giggles and snide remarks of a drill, there was a clear aura of fear. During that forty-five seconds, many students were in a state of shock and couldn't say anything. At least two students called out my name in such a way as to suggest I need to come to their desk right *now* and save them. A few uttered the Lord's name, and a few others burst forth with a frightened outcry of sorts. During this time, I was constantly talking to the students from under my desk and through that four-inch space I previously mentioned, "It will end soon, students! Don't worry, this building was built to withstand an earthquake! You'll be okay! You're safe under your desks!"

It's remarkable how much one can say in forty-five seconds. Most of what I said, however, was designed to help me convince myself that I would live to see another day. Because, truth be told, I was horror-struck!

When it finally ended, I instructed everyone to get back in their seats. The students were deadly quiet, and their eyes were huge, looking to me as to how they should react. Since everyone was fine, and there was no noticeable physical damage to the room, I decided a little humor might work best.

"Okay, students, wasn't that just special? I couldn't have created a ride at Disneyland better that that!"

The last drill we practiced every month was the lockdown drill. This would occur if there was some compelling reason for locking our doors. Maybe there was a dangerous, rabid, frothing dog on campus or a sociopathic criminal nearby. Maybe an enraged parent had just left the main office, saying, "Fuck you all, I'm going to kill someone." Or maybe someone spotted a student wielding a handgun and out to get revenge on the school bully. Whatever the case may be, a lockdown would be necessary, and an announcement over the intercom would signal its beginning.

Now, there were two levels of lockdown, and both were practiced. One level involved a low-level threat, where I would simply lock my door and continue teaching. Maybe a bank robber was in the general area, and we'd do this as a precaution. The other level was considered more serious. Not only would I lock the door, but I'd move all the students to the corner of the room where they would be hidden from any intruder who might be on campus or even inside the building. If the intruder happened to look through the small classroom door window, he would see no one and thus continue his murderous rampage to the next room where human bodies may be ripe for rifling bullets through.

Now, don't get me wrong. I'm not trying to make fun of these drills, based on the fact that there have been many school shootings in the recent past. But statistically, it's highly unlikely anything bad will happen. I still drive my car, for example, even though fatal car accidents happen every hour of every day. It's a calculated risk we all take. So when an actual, real lockdown was announced over the intercom one fine day, I took it with a grain of salt.

The principal came over the intercom and announced a lockdown but failed to indicate the level. I remember I was in the middle of something semi-interesting in class: the discussion of a poem. So I concluded it was a lower-level lockdown, calmly walked over to the door, locked it, and resumed the lesson.

About two minutes passed when I heard some muffled sounds coming from the window slit in the door. I looked toward the door and saw the vice principal's head and shoulders through the window. She was clearly agitated and moving about wildly. I saw her mouth busily shifting and chattering through the window slit but could not make out a word due to the thickness of the glass. Her mousy brown hair was flailing about, and her pearl necklace was jumping up and down. She looked like a mime gone mad, pressing her open hands up against an imaginary wall...or could the crazed intruder be chasing her, and the closest safe haven was my room? In case the latter were true, I raced to the door and opened it.

"Mr. Wong," she frantically blasted, "this is a serious lockdown! You need to get your students in the corner of your classroom *now*! *We have criminals on campus!*"

Well, she announced these words in a serious and loud manner while her face was contorting in every which way. Saliva was being ejected from her mouth like an errant water hose, and her eyes were fireballs of fright, twitching and darting about.

I closed the door, made sure it's locked, and instructed my kids to get in the corner of the room. Now, due to the vice principal's terrifying announcement, the students became scared shitless. They envisioned a 1999 Columbine High School shooting or the 2012 Sandy Hook Elementary School tragedy. They huddled in the corner, some whispering words of comfort to their friends. Others were crying out to me for help.

"*Help!* Mr. Wong, what should we do? Oh my God! Are we going to die? I need to call my mom! I need to go to the bathroom! I think it's too late!"

Now, our vice principal, whom I will call Mrs. Stein, was an easily irritable sort of person. She became overly excited at the smallest of situations and reacted to them with much emotion. Her clammy hands and fingers trembled and flew about with every syllable uttered. So when she appeared at my door in such a dramatic fashion, I knew I needed to be the calming force. She had successfully caused my students to be as frightened and agitated as she was, which I guess speaks to her respectability. But the problem now was that I had twenty-six alarmed and terrified students huddled in the corner of the room. Once again, I thought a dose of humor might be the antidote to their frightened state of mind.

"Okay, students," I calmly began, "if anyone breaks down the door and starts shooting, everyone needs to quickly get behind me since I am confident my blubber can absorb at least fifty rounds of ammunition."

It took a few seconds for students to digest what I just said, and then I heard a few giggles. Most, however, were still too traumatized by the situation, and their heightened sense of insecurity masked any humorous interpretation. So I felt I needed to reach out to them again, "Students, listen to me. One of the things I've cleared with all of your parents is your family's life insurance policies. Don't worry, if you are gunned down, your parents and siblings will be financially set for life."

Still, a few students were staring at me blankly, scared as hell, and looking for something they could hang on to and understand, so I tried one more time, "Students, if we do not survive this venture, the good news is that we'll all go to heaven together under the direction of me, your loyal teacher. And I'll be honored to lead you to the promised land."

Well, I guess this caused the remaining skeptical students to snap out of it. This statement was apparently too disgusting for them to fathom, and the overall negative mood was lifted. Some even began laughing, which quieted and calmed others who were just now accepting the predicament as relatively safe.

About ten minutes later, an announcement came over the intercom that the lockdown was over. I guess two men had robbed the 7-Eleven close to the school and had ran across our baseball field, with the police in hot pursuit.

Anyway, I resumed my engaging discussion of a poem by Edgar Allen Poe called "The Raven," which was much less scary to the students than what had just occurred. The lockdown had deflated, by comparison, Poe's wonderful words of horror, forevermore.

Chapter 12

Minority Madness

On the roof of a very tall building are four men. One is Asian, one is Mexican, one is Black, and one is white. The Asian walks to the ledge and says, "This is for my people!" and jumps off the roof. The Mexican then walks to the ledge and says, "This is for my people!" and jumps off the roof. Next is the Black guy's turn. He walks to the ledge and says, "This is for my people!" and throws the white guy off the roof.

When I first started teaching in 1979, "Affirmative Action" was a seriously popular government policy. Affirmative Action meant that large employers must hire minorities and women if their ratio for these two categories didn't meet federal standards. The thinking was that if the US population was 15 percent African American, and only 2 percent of your employees were African American, then you were a racist, and you better start hiring some Black folks real quick. Affirmative Action, therefore, was supposed to end discrimination in hiring practices and give *all* people a fair chance to work.

So school districts were actively seeking minorities to hire in order to meet government guidelines. Lucky for me, my last name was *Wong*, the most common Chinese name in the world. This meant I was a bona fide minority, and I would get preferential treatment when considered for a job.

In the high school I first taught at, there were eight social studies teachers, and they were all males and white. So I came along to bring some color to the soup. Shortly after I was hired, I asked the social studies department head, who was on the interview team, if I had been hired because of Affirmative Action.

I remember him smiling slightly and, with a tinge of embarrassment in his voice, said, "Well, Roger, you were the only minority who applied. We were hoping for a minority who was also female, to kill two birds with one stone as they say. But we figured that one out of two wasn't too bad."

So at this time, I must officially thank my father, who was 100 percent Chinese descendant. He was an immigrant from Southern China and came to America as a teenager. He fought in World War II, was employed as an electrician most of his life, and was one of the many Horatio Alger success stories in America. He worked hard and did very well for himself and his family.

But I was only half of a minority. My mother was 100 percent white, a Norwegian American who lived in Fargo, North Dakota. So that left me 50 percent minority—which, I guess, is good enough for government work.

Being half Asian, with slightly darker skin and black hair, caused a very intriguing and curious racial experience for me growing up. People looked at me and just were not quite sure what I was. Some thought I was Caucasian with a slight tan. Most would guess Hispanic or Native American. A few were keen enough to see some Asian in me. I have had, believe it or not, one person who thought I was a light-skinned African American. It happened when I was sitting at a motorcycle bar on a "Taco Tuesday" afternoon. I struck up a conversation with an African American gentleman sitting in the stool next to me. We were chatting for maybe fifteen minutes when, all of a sudden, his facial expression took a puzzling turn. He paused, looked me up and down, and very sincerely asked, "Are you a brother?"

I answered that I was not, but I thanked him ardently and informed him that because of his conclusion that I was Black, I have now been taken, at one time or another, for *all* five races. He became somewhat bewildered at my comment. Yet he smiled and responded by revealing to me that he's *always* been taken as Black, and there hasn't been much fun in that!

When I taught middle school, I often had fun asking my students what race they thought I belonged to. (Most middle schoolers are too dumb—excuse me, too naive—to know *Wong* is Asian.) More often than not, they are shocked to find out I'm half Asian and half white. And interestingly enough, my wife, upon first meeting me, thought I was Samoan. She thought Samoan guys were hot, I assume, and was taken aback to find out my true racial background. It was okay with her, though, as long as I "looked" Samoan, so we continued dating and eventually married.

Nevertheless, I've been discriminated against many times in my life. For example, in high school, a particular girl I was infatuated with couldn't go out with me due to her parents' prejudices. I've been called "chink" and been stereotyped by people of all ages. They envisioned me going home to eat a dinner of rice and chow mein, attending my gung fu class, and sleeping on my bamboo mat. They assumed I knew Bruce Lee personally and, just for the fun of it, sang "Ching Chong Chinamen" in a high voice. That always added a humorous touch to our conversations.

But I must admit I have enjoyed the many advantages of being a minority in America as well. As I said earlier, I probably would not have been hired as a teacher if not for my 50 percent claim to Asian ancestry. And an assertion of racial discrimination, in many situations, tend to get you the desired outcome. In fact, employers, or people in positions of power, know an alleged act of racial discrimination can get you a very expensive lawsuit or some very bad press. This was why I, along with other minority teachers, were pretty comfortable and secure in our positions. A white administrator will hesitate to mess with us. The idea of firing a minority teacher is almost out of the question, given the backlash of being accused of discrimination. And giving a minority teacher a bad evaluation can be potentially problematic as well.

It was my thirty-fourth year of teaching—my very *last* year of "touching the future," as I often put it. Every year, teachers get evaluated by the principal or vice principal. During my first thirty-three years, I've always earned an exemplary evaluation. Statements like "very effective teaching techniques," "challenges students to achieve academic goals," and "highly knowledgeable about subject matter," littered my final evaluations every year—that is, every year except my last.

The vice principal in charge of evaluating me was a white female, and I'll call her Ms. Schuster. She meant well but was overly excited about all the new educational reforms cascading down upon teachers. It just so happened that during my last few years of teaching, the new instructional techniques that *all* teachers were supposed to wholeheartedly embrace involved cooperative learning. This meant we put students into small groups. From here, the students would be encouraged to "discover," on their own, answers or solutions to subject-related questions. This would lead to fun projects involving posters, artwork, video productions, and it would all culminate in a wonderful group multimedia presentation in front of the super interested classroom students. Sounds great, but this kind of stuff was *not* effective for a large number of students. It also took *way* too much class time. And in the end, the students who were listening to the culminating multimedia presentations were sleeping. So as an experienced teacher, I continued to teach with methods I knew worked. Unfortunately, as a result, I earned my first bad evaluation.

According to Ms. Schuster, my instruction needed updating. It was old-fashioned. The "sit down, shut up, and get to work" approach to classroom management no longer applied to today's youth. I needed to welcome into my instructional repertoire the current "proven" techniques. So I did the only logical thing anyone in my position would do: accuse her of *racism*. I didn't use that exact word, but it was pretty clear what I was saying when I confronted Ms. Schuster after finding out, according to her, my classroom instruction sucked.

"Ms. Schuster, I've learned through the many years I've taught that what I do is very effective for myself and my students. In fact, my students standardized test scores are significantly higher than the other teachers. I don't understand, therefore, how I could get dinged on 'instruction,' especially after thirty-three years of excellent evaluations."

Ms. Schuster reacted with a bountiful burst of laughter and replied, "Mr. Wong, test scores are not everything!"

Now you have to realize—if you were not a teacher in 2013—that, in fact, test scores *were everything*. The standardized test results associated with a school determined (in the eyes of the federal government, the state, and the school district) whether the school was fit to continue as a school, period. If scores were low, the school would be labeled as a bad school. It had bad teachers, bad administrators, bad cafeteria food, and ugly school colors. So when Ms. Schuster so delightfully and straightforwardly maintained that test scores didn't matter, I knew I was dealing with a no-win situation brought on by an out-of-touch, suck-up administrator. She was much more concerned about having the teachers under her conform to the newest instructional fad. So I fired the only thing left in my diminished arsenal—racism.

"Ms. Schuster, test scores are very, very important, as you should know. In fact, since my students score high on the standardized tests, what difference does it make *how* I instruct my kids? I could show them cartoons all day, as long as their test scores are high. I just don't get it. I'm wondering if you are confusing bad instruction with something else, like how I do my bulletin boards, the way my desk is organized, or my background."

There it is! Did you notice how slyly and unobtrusively I slipped in that word—*background?* Yes, I was thinking to myself, she needs to know I believe that she's giving me a bad mark on instruction because she's a racist!

When Ms. Schuster heard that vital, weighty word, her facial expression transformed from one of confidence to one of fearful nervousness. Her bubbly body language shifted and drooped.

"Huh, okay, Mr. Wong, let me think about this over the weekend. And I'll get back with you on Monday."

On Monday, I was called into her office. I was fully prepared to use stronger euphemisms for *background* if I needed to. She got right to the point and humbly articulated the following:

"You know, Mr. Wong, I thought a lot about this over the weekend. In fact, it was the *only* thing I thought about over the weekend. And I've decided to change your bad mark to a good one."

Thank you, Dad! Thank you so much for being a race other than white in this great land of ours!

Chapter 13

The Achievement Crap

Can't we all just get along?

—Rodney King

There's institutional racism running rampant in the hallways of today's public schools. Teachers and administrators are discriminating against minority students and robbing them of their right to an equal education. The land of equality and justice is in jeopardy! In education, the Civil Rights Movement of the 1960s has been forgotten and tossed aside. Those goddamn white supremacist teachers ought to be shackled! And we have proof that this is happening: the achievement gap!

Okay, settle down, and take a deep breath, and let me first explain the "achievement gap." The achievement gap refers to the fact that standardized test scores show that most minority students score significantly lower than Caucasian students. Specifically, white students score the highest followed closely by Asian students. Then there is a sizable gap in scores between the two aforementioned racial groups and African Americans, Hispanics, and Native Americans. The conclusion, therefore, is that there is some serious racism going on in schools, and it must be fixed. This is one of the many current "reforms" in education today. And teachers, for the most part, are responsible for solving this obvious inequality.

As of 2013, the quaint country of Finland led the world in international student test scores, so there was a lot of educational buzz about how they are able to achieve this. One variable that was pointed out to me by a counselor at my school, when I mentioned this to her, was that the main reason Finland's student scores are so high is that they have a homogeneous society. I don't think she was referring to "culturally" homogeneous, either, since we were framing our conversation around the achievement gap problem in America. So what she meant was that Finland's population is predominately white, and that's why their test scores were so high. When I told her (half jokingly, half seriously), that it was actually a racist statement, she was taken aback a bit, especially as a trusted staff member who counsels kids. I then told her that I agree, to a certain extent, with her assessment as to why Finland's test scores are the highest and related to her the following anecdote:

I had a principal at the middle school I taught at whom I trusted and became good friends with. So I felt comfortable with him when I half kiddingly requested an all-Asian class. It was obvious to him (and everyone) why I wanted this. I'd have, overall, a highly motivated, intelligent, hardworking group of students. What teacher wouldn't want this? In essence, I'd have a homogeneous classroom and subsequently create some pretty high test scores, just like Finland. Because of this idea, some people would call me a racist—except, according to some people's definition, I can't be a racist, because I'm not white (LOL). But that's another whole issue, which can be discussed and either defended or ridiculed by you at some other time.

Anyway, while I was teaching, I often thought about how the achievement gap could be eliminated since we do want everyone to be equal in America. And I came up with a foolproof solution! Unfortunately, when I presented my solution to a select number of teachers, I was *not* received very warmly.

My first concern was that, as we were raising the test scores of the Hispanic, African American, and Native American students, what were we supposed to do with the Caucasians and Asians? Most of my teaching career, I found myself with a wonderful mixture of students. And I always thought my goal was to make sure *all* students learned. The achievement gap problem, then, would always be present. As the African American scores went up, so would the white test scores. As the Hispanic scores excelled, so would the Asian test scores. It was truly a conundrum!

Then it hit me. In order to narrow, or eliminate, the gap in test scores, we needed to slow down or stop the progress of the whites and Asians in order to give the other three racial groups a fair chance at catching up. As I so confidently proposed to the teachers at my school, the solution to the achievement gap was quite simple. All we needed to do was direct the Caucasian and Asian students to the cafeteria every day. While there, they would enjoy the school day by watching movies, making sure the movies had no educational value. With this group, the school district would need only one staff member for every hundred or so students for supervision purposes. After all, they would be just watching popular movies. They would be totally engaged.

Then, with the African American, Hispanic, and Native American students, we could drastically reduce class size and student-teacher ratio, which is one of the time honored, proven ways of increasing student learning. In fact, at some schools across this great nation, these students may receive one-on-one tutoring all day! Then, after a determined period of time, students would be tested. We would continue this process until all racial groups are scoring similarly on the standardized tests. Achievement gap problem solved!

My school could be the first to implement this unique program. I would lead the charge, since it was my idea! Pretty soon, the news of my school's success would spread across the nation. We would be a model for other schools to replicate. We'll get local, state, and national accolades, and I would make big bucks traveling across the country, illustrating and detailing the procedures necessary to end this despicable achievement gap, this den of racial inequality. Since schools were currently "data driven," I'd have all the necessary statistics and information at hand and present them to the rather large audiences in a colorful PowerPoint presentation. I'd write a book.

I'd get numerous speaking engagements and be the preferred guest on talk shows. I might, given enough time, get a monument next to Martin Luther King Jr. in Washington, DC! Oh, how I love today's educational reforms!

Chapter 14

Freaky Happenings

Student: Teacher, is there life after death?
Teacher: Why do you ask?
Student: I may need the extra time to finish all this homework
you gave us.

Sometimes, some very freaky things happen in class. When I say *freaky*, I mean weird, bizarre, unexplainable, and semiscary—in a Stephen King kind of way. In particular, there were two occasions in class where I thought I was in the "Twilight Zone," literally, and my heart was racing, fueled by a strong dose of confounding trepidation.

For about six years, in the 1980s, I taught sociology and psychology in high school. As a rather young teacher at the time, I was thrilled to have the privilege of teaching these courses. Usually, these kinds of classes in high school were reserved for the social studies department head, but for some unknown reason, he didn't want to do it. Since I was a history and sociology major in college, this was a perfect fit for me. I had also taken several psychology courses in college, and these topics were extremely interesting to me, and I was ready to bring that enthusiasm to my students. Furthermore, these classes were electives for the upperclassmen, meaning for the juniors and seniors, so my students would be highly motivated, mature, and college-bound. They couldn't wait to get another academic credit under their belts. Truly, I've never had classes so enjoyable to teach.

Anyway, the school district supplied me with a very good high school–level textbook for the psychology course. I spent the good part of that first summer reading it, choosing which chapters to cover, and making lesson plans. One of the more intriguing chapters was titled "Altered States of Consciousness." And it was from this chapter that a couple of freaky occurrences took place in class.

One of the topics up for discussion was sleeping and dreaming. I'd cover, with my students, the stages of sleep, REM (rapid eye movement) sleep, and a bit on dream interpretation. As part of my preparation for this lesson, I had looked up some documented—unusual but supposedly true—cases of sleeping and dreaming. I could use them as attention-getters to start my lesson. One of these cases involved the idea that dreams sometimes come true. The reason for dreams coming true may be pure coincidence or one's ability to predict the future, if you are inclined to believe in that kind of stuff. I always let the students make their own decision as to which one was the truth. Anyway, there are some fascinating "true cases" involving certain people who have had dreams that actually come true. And I loved expounding these to the class as a way of starting off the lesson.

In this one particular case, a man never had any unusual dreaming issues, until his father passed away. Then, his father would come into his dreams and tell him things that would happen in the future. Most of the father's predictions were rather insignificant happenings. He might tell him that, in a week, his son would come home from school with an A on his arithmetic test and be very excited about it. And it would happen. He'd predict that his wife, next Tuesday, would be home an hour late from work due to congestion on the freeway. And it would happen. He would tell him he'd get an unexpected raise at work next month, and it would happen.

At first, the son was skeptical about what his father told him in his dreams, but literally, *everything* he said came true in real life. After a few months, he was a believer in what his father would tell him and would even pass on some of the predictions to his family members.

The family members quickly became believers as well, as they also realized that every prediction did, in fact, come to be. After a few years of this, the father's forecasts were taken for granted, and they became a normal part of the family's life. The prophecies came true every single time, whether they were negative or positive happenings, and the family members simply took it as inevitable, future events.

Then one night, his father came into his dream to tell him something rather portentous, alarming, and astonishing. He told his son that, in about six months, he would die from a freak accident. Now, the son *knew* this would happen, just as all the hundreds of other predictions happened. So he told his family. They immediately went through the grieving process, and they began making arrangements for his demise. They increased his life insurance, planned for the funeral, and discussed the family's future financial situation after his eminent death. Well, as foreseen, he was involved in an atypical, unprecedented accident at work about six months later and pronounced dead.

Now, I was recounting this "true," scientifically documented case to the students with much zest and zeal. The students were totally absorbed in the story and were in a state of unadulterated wonder and amazement. I always ended the narrative with this closing statement: "So as you can see, class, I guess there are some people who do, in fact, have dreams that come true."

At this juncture, there was usually a delay of ten to fifteen seconds where students were still digesting this remarkable story. I waited for the immense effect of the story to diminish so that students could properly comment or ask questions. On this one occasion, however, I noticed a girl toward the back of the room who didn't look amazed, excited, or surprised at all. Instead, she looked totally terrified. She was frozen to her seat, with her eyes dilated, wide open, and gazing through me. Clearly, she was highly disturbed by the story and extremely uncomfortable with my chronicle of dreams coming true.

Now, this particular girl was an A student, rather quiet, and serious about her studies. She didn't goof around or play practical jokes, and her demeanor was true to her cordial intentions. It was halfway through the year at this time, and I had never known her to be anything other than honest, trustworthy, and sincere. I'll call her Debra.

So when I noticed Debra in an obvious state of discomfort during this ten-to-fifteen-second interlude, I felt compelled to find out what was going on with her.

"Huh, Debra, are you okay back there?"

"Um…Um…Mr. Wong, well, I guess I'm okay…but your story sort of freaked me out."

"Really? Why is that, Debra?"

Attempting to gather her composure and with a hesitant, yet unflinching tone of voice, Debra continued, "Well, ever since I can remember, my dreams have also come true."

At this point, I was not particularly alarmed or surprised. I figured she was just overly absorbed in the story and maybe recalled one time where she had dreamed something like she had received a compliment from her parents about her grades and then did in real life. You know, something that is pretty vague and obviously a coincidence. So I decided to pursue it a bit longer to hopefully show her that her reaction to my true story was not equitable to her experience, that she was overreacting and needed to calm down. The story from the psychology journal was not, in any significant way, identical to her dreaming incidences.

"Okay, Debra, I was wondering if you could give me an example of what you mean when you say your dreams also come true."

"Um, okay, Mr. Wong. Well, last night I had a dream where I was in your class."

"Really?" I interrupted. "Well, I'm sure if I surveyed the class, it's very possible many people in this class have had a dream where they were in my class…[attempting to insert some humor]…and it probably was a nightmare!" One kid in the front row laughed, and two others eked out a smile.

"No, Mr. Wong, I'm dead serious!" Debra emphasized. "Last night, I had a dream where I was in your class, and *everything* you said, up until now, was said by you in my dream *word for word*. This happens to me all the time. I had originally thought that everyone did this. But now I know I'm not normal. What's wrong with me, Mr. Wong?"

On another occasion in psychology class, we were discussing paranormal activity, things like ESP (extra sensory perception) and other hard-to-explain phenomena. Again, I had previously looked through psychology journals for "true" cases of people with documented experiences in this area and used them to start the lesson. I was gesticulating to the class about cases of near-death experiences, out-of-body experiences, and angels and letting the class know that some people have claimed to have died, visited heaven, and returned with the ability to describe it. In the documented cases of afterlife experiences, there seemed to be three characteristics common among all of the cases. First, there was an intense feeling of peace and contentment upon death; next, they described traveling through a tunnel-like structure, and third, they recalled encountering a bright, warm, enveloping light at the end of the tunnel. Those who were religious interpreted this light as Jesus or God. Those who were not religious just saw it as an awesome, all-encompassing, tranquil light. Either way, they did not want to leave this place but were drawn back to physical life for some unknown reason. Thus, they were able to recount exactly what happened to them after their passing.

I also related to my students about people who claim to have angels or entities around them. It appears to be more common among the very young, who have open minds and tell their parents about their "invisible" friend. The parents usually pass it off as an overactive imagination. And it's also common among the very old, who may be close to death, and claim to see apparitions, or glimpses, of the afterlife. I hate to say it, but prior to my own father's death, my dad swore he "battled" with the devil in his living room, and my dad was the most logical, practical, and realistic man I have ever known. It was hard *not* to believe him.

Anyway, I was excitedly telling true occurrences of this nature to my students as a way to gain their interest for the lesson that day. I usually ended the stories with this closing statement: "So as you can see, students, there may be people out there who really have seen angels or other spirits who talk to them or relate to them in some way."

Once again, the students were usually fully engaged with what I had told them and needed a few seconds to absorb the totality of what they had just heard.

While relating this information to the students, however, I noticed a student—whom I will call Fernando—smiling at me the entire time I was speaking. At first, I thought he was mocking me and laughing at the perceived absurdity of having invisible friends or angel acquaintances. But Fernando was a straight-arrow kind of guy, not prone to being a jerk. He was known to be a nice guy, honest, and had many friends in the class. Anyway, Fernando raised his hand upon the end of my final statement, and I was quite curious as to what his comment might be.

"Yes, Fernando. You have a question or comment?"

"Well, yes, Mr. Wong. Actually, what you have been talking about really hits home with me. I have an invisible friend, whom I believe is my guardian angel. I am the only one who can see him. His name is Ricky, and he comes to me often and gives me some excellent advice."

"Oh, really?" I hesitantly responded, thinking, at first, he was playing some sort of sick practical joke. But then I realized that this was not the case based on his body language, matter-of-fact tone of voice, and knowledge of his personality.

Furthermore, just then, the student sitting next to Fernando interjected, "Yes, Mr. Wong. It's true. Fernando is my best friend, and I spend a lot of time at his house. I hate to say it, but I believe Ricky is real even though I personally have never seen him."

"Um…okay," I uttered, trying to stay calm and focused, "so, Fernando, when was the last time you saw Ricky?"

"Mr. Wong, I see him right now. He's sitting on the desk in front of me."

Now, the desk in front of Fernando was empty. Everyone, except Fernando, saw that it was vacant, yet Fernando swore Ricky, his angel, was sitting there. In an attempt to get more information, I then asked Fernando to tell the class what Ricky looked like and what kind of advice he gave him. Fernando began to answer my inquiry with much exhilaration and passion but abruptly stopped. Taken aback at his sudden cessation, I asked Fernando why he had stopped.

Fernando turned sullen and responded, "Well, Mr. Wong, Ricky is not here anymore. He left."

"Why?" I humbly inquired.

"Ricky doesn't like to be talked about. He told me he doesn't like to be the center of attention. He's not super happy right now. But that's okay. I'll see him tonight and apologize."

Chapter 15

A Quiet Classroom

Silence is golden...unless you have
kids, then silence is suspicious.

I decided, while attending college in 1976, to spend fifty precious dollars to learn how to meditate, transcendental meditation style. TM was quite fashionable at this time. The Maharishi Mahesh Yogi had developed it in the 1950s, and the Beatles had popularized it in the 1970s.

TM came with some pretty amazing claims. It alleged that if you did this simple technique twice a day for twenty minutes each, you'd be healthier and happier. They proclaimed some specific rewards as well. Your blood pressure would go down, if it was high. If you were really busy, it would help because you'd need fewer hours of sleep. And if you were a student, your grades would improve. So for $50, I thought this was a pretty good deal.

TM training first involved a few short seminars to give us some general information about TM. They imparted to us about its history, its benefits, and how it worked. Many were curious about this last part. How could such a simple technique cause all these wonderful things to happen? So we asked. The instructor smiled and was eager to tell us, but there was a problem. We needed to know a lot about quantum physics in order for us to fully understand how it worked. Unfortunately, none of us did, so we just took his word for it.

Finally, the day arrived where I'd actually learn the technique. But during this whole process, I became a bit skeptical. The claims were rather outrageous, and the surroundings smacked of religion. The Maharishi's picture was everywhere, and fresh flowers adorned every available crevice of the early 1900s house they had occupied near the university. I halfheartedly believed I was getting myself indoctrinated into some kind of eerie cult.

They were nice to me up until this point, but would they now put me in a trance and ask me to give my soul to their cause? Would I, next week, be wearing a white robe and sitting with my legs crossed as I chanted and handed out TM leaflets to people at the airport?

My instructor, however, was clean shaven and wore a suit and tie. That helped ease my concerns a little bit. But he sat me in front of what looked very much like an altar. There was the picture of the Maharishi smiling, and fresh flowers on both sides of it. He then approached the altar and lit some incense. He next began "talking" to Maharishi's picture, but I couldn't understand what he was saying. It was either gibberish or Hindu words, I'm not sure which. This went on for about sixty seconds. Now I began to worry. This was creepy, but I was curious as to what might happen next. Next, he turned to me and asked me to sit comfortably in the chair and close my eyes. He then gave me my mantra, which he said several times so as to make sure I had it right. He told me to repeat this mantra to myself while sitting in the chair. So I did.

Then a very peculiar thing happened. I became immediately very "high." I smiled broadly because it was unexpected, and it was a very awesome feeling. It felt like my brain was being massaged from within. My brain was being tickled and warmed, it seemed. It was quite wonderful!

So I practiced TM throughout my college years, and their claims actually materialized for me. I was in great health during this time, happy, and my grades improved. I was a mere B student in high school with a cumulative GPA of 3.2, taking the easiest courses

I could. In college, however, I ended up summa cum laude with a 3.7 GPA, taking much harder courses.

After analyzing it, though, I think the explanation is pretty simple. Basically, TM gives you a deep rest twice a day. A well-rested person is usually healthier, happier, and can focus much better in class. *How* or *why* it gives you that deep rest, however, is something for quantum physics to explain, evidently.

After college, though, I quit doing TM. They started making some scientifically impossible claims. They said that, through advanced TM practice, you could levitate. And their proof was a video of TM practitioners bouncing up and down from a legs-folded sitting position. I decided to get out while the getting was good.

Anyway, my TM experience became yet another lesson for my psychology students in high school. Again, the placement of this lesson fit well with the "Altered States of Consciousness" chapter in the textbook.

The lesson started with me giving students the basic information: What is TM? What are its benefits? How does it work? etc. Then, for fun, I was going to teach them how to do it using *my* mantra.

Now, telling anyone your mantra was strictly forbidden. My original TM instructor had made that perfectly clear: "Under no circumstances, Roger, should you reveal your mantra to anyone, ever."

I guess it was like TM suicide, or something. We even signed a paper agreeing to never divulge our mantra to anyone, including spouses or family members. This was serious business.

But they never explained why we couldn't, and it seemed sort of silly, like keeping a meaningless secret. Plus, I hadn't practiced TM for years and felt the statute of limitations had elapsed on whatever I had signed. I thought it would simply be a very interesting exercise for the students.

So one fine February day, I addressed the class thusly, "Okay, students, now we're going to learn how to meditate by using the transcendental meditation technique. First, sit comfortably in your seats. Make sure your whole body is comfortable, including your legs and arms. You may want to fold your arms on your lap. Now, close your eyes, and be completely quiet and still. Start saying to yourself this sound, *I-ang-ga*. Let me repeat it so that you will be saying it to yourself correctly, *I-ang-ga*. You will continue to say this to yourself. It doesn't have to be said at any particular pace. If you discover you have stopped saying it, that's okay. Just start saying it again. We will do this for about twenty minutes. I'll keep track of the time so you can concentrate on the mantra. Okay, once again, the mantra is *I-ang-ga*. And begin…"

So I now had twenty-five students, and myself, sitting absolutely quiet in our seats. Our hands were folded in our laps, and our heads were slightly tilted down. About thirty seconds into our meditative state, a student, who worked in the office, opened the classroom door. He saw what's going on (absolutely nothing!) and was visibly perplexed and disturbed. He stopped in midstride and stretched out his nervous hand that contained a note. I looked up and gently took it from him and nodded my head slightly, as a signal for him to leave. He did so by tiptoeing away. He stopped at the door to take one last long look before he slowly turned the doorknob so as not to disturb whatever the hell was going on.

I looked to see if this office worker's presence had affected any of my students, but it hadn't. They were still sitting there in their meditative positions, quiet, eyes closed, and heads tilted. Maybe they were experiencing that "high" I had previously described and wasn't going to let this idiot ruin it.

But now, I began thinking about what this student office worker might say to Mrs. Simpson, our office secretary, and how it might cause alarm. Would the principal come storming down to my classroom, demanding to know what I was teaching and why? Would he think of me as crazy and put a letter in my file? I was hoping not, and I was pretty sure the school staff knew me too well. So the student learned more about Mr. Wong that day when he returned to the office excitedly ready to tell Mrs. Simpson what he had just observed.

"Hey, Mrs. Simpson!" he declared excitedly and out of breath, "you won't believe what I saw when I delivered the note to Mr. Wong's class!"

"Oh, really? What did you see, Curtis?" Mrs. Simpson responded with a prying yet skeptical tone.

"Well, I walk in, and everyone is just sitting there, with their hands folded in complete silence, including Mr. Wong."

"*Mmm*, well, you know Mr. Wong likes it quiet in there."

"Yes, but they weren't *doing* anything. They weren't reading or writing or anything!"

"Really? Well, you know Mr. Wong really likes it quiet in there."

Frustrated, Curtis turned away just as Mrs. Scranton, the school nurse, was coming out of her adjacent office.

"Hey, Mrs. Scranton!" Curtis shouted with much enthusiastic desperation.

"Yes," Mrs. Scranton replied.

"You won't believe this, but I was just in Mr. Wong's class, and the students were absolutely quiet. It almost looked like Mr. Wong had put them into some sort of trance, or they were praying or half unconscious. You should go take a look."

"Okay, maybe I will, I need to relax a bit. I've had a hard day so far. And I know Mr. Wong likes it quiet in there."

Chapter 16

A Hairy Situation

You've got bad eating habits if you use a grocery cart in 7-Eleven, okay?

—Dennis Miller

What's the grossest thing you have ever eaten? Snails? Frog's legs? Chicken feet? "Prairie Oysters" or bull's testicles? Maybe you've accidentally swallowed some urine.

Although I have no memory of this, my brother, who is two years younger than me, claims he tasted my pee when I whizzed on him in the bathtub when we were around six and four years old. He said he was surprised at the sweet and salty taste. Why was I urinating on him in the bathtub? Because as the older, stronger brother, I guess I could!

I've heard, in fact, that in some extreme situations, people will voluntarily drink their own pee if they are stranded in the desert or are in some predicament where they cannot get liquids any other way. I know, it's gross! But I'm sure most of you, older brothers (and older sisters), know what I'm talking about, and you may have even more disgusting and mean things you put your little brother or sister through. It's a sad but true reality of growing up with older siblings.

I even see this pattern of behavior with my two handsome grandsons, who are about one and one half years apart in age. The oldest boy drops toys on his youngest brother's head, steals from him, rolls over him with his entire body weight, hits him, and does a myriad of other potentially injurious and consistently intentional actions upon a helpless toddler. So I guess not much has changed in the last half century.

Anyway, as mentioned in earlier chapters, there was a sixteen-year period when the staff at the middle school I taught at was very tight. There was a group of us, numbering around eight, who spent significant amounts of time with each other after school hours. We took trips and partied together. We attended each other's family functions and celebrated holidays at each other's houses. When kids were getting married, we were invited. I think you get the picture—we were close friends and shared a lot of good times.

And some of this fun involved playing practical jokes on each other at school. I personally felt a little uncomfortable playing a practical joke on my colleague-friends, but I was always "in the know" about the planning and execution of the jokes of others but never responsible for the possible repercussions afterward. I'd just sit back and watch the hilarity ensue. Yet I was rarely the object of the next appalling frolic into the wacky world of mockery and misery. It was a wise and safe position to be in.

Once a practical joke was finalized and fulfilled, subsequent plans by the "jokee" would be set in motion for retaliatory satisfaction, and the expectation was that this new joke would be bigger, better, more ingenious, and with a consequence that truly surprises, shames, and astounds everyone. Here were some of the practical jokes some of the teachers at my school endured:

- Our principal was leaving for vacation out of state one Friday and took his luggage to school as he had to rush straight from school to the airport. A teacher somehow was able to get into his suitcase and placed a petrified rat inside.
- Open house is the day when parents visit the school in the evening to talk to his or her kid's teachers. Teachers were

supposed to inform parents about curriculum, grading, and classroom policies. Most teachers at my school stayed after school, prepared their room for the parents, and then left for home or for dinner. They returned to school just before open house began, usually around 7:00 PM. On this particular day, a teacher put a Budweiser girl's poster on another teacher's bulletin board. He made sure it was stapled to the *back* bulletin board so the teacher's chances of seeing it, when arriving just before open house began, was unlikely. When parents arrived, however, they would definitely notice it, and the teacher might have some explaining to do.

- At another open house, a teacher got into the room of another teacher and carefully chose a few words on his front board to purposely misspell. For example, he might change *receive* to *recieve* or *schedule* to *schedual*. It's improbable the teacher would notice this, but the parents would! And he would have some explaining to do, especially as a language arts teacher.

- One late night, a bunch of teachers "foiled" the principal's office. This means that every item in his office—large or small, from his desk to his individual pencils—were wrapped in aluminum foil. It took hours and hours. But when the principal arrived the next morning, his expression was priceless!

- On several occasions, this particular rotund, gaseous social studies teacher would enter his colleague-friend's classroom while he was teaching, under the pretense of asking a question. Then he'd let go with a silent but toxic blowout of excremental stench. He'd quickly scoot out of the room, leaving a most grotesque scent for the unfortunates left inside to enjoy. This same teacher would enter his coteacher friend's classroom, say nothing, and spontaneously and unexpectedly turn over his garbage can and then quickly leave.

- On several occasions, rotten cheese, or other obnoxious, putrid things, were placed in teacher's desks over the weekend.

- A teacher coerced his sister to call the principal, pretending to be an employee of a bank. She cleverly and underhandedly explained to the principal that he had $190,000 waiting to be claimed from an investment he had made twenty-five years ago but had been long forgotten. She was so convincing that the principal was overjoyed, thinking he had won the equivalent to the state lottery.

- A photo of our school district's superintendent was taped to the inside of a urinal in the men's faculty restroom. Thus, you either had to piss on the big boss or handle a urine-drenched picture trying to remove it. Most whizzed on the boss.

- Many times, when a teacher was absent, this same aforementioned rotund social studies teacher would make sure the students knew the reason for his absence. The conversation would go something like this:

Teacher: Okay, class, Mr. Zester is absent today, as you know. I hope he's okay. Quite frankly, I'm a bit worried about him.

Student: How come? What's wrong?

Teacher: Well, he had a very, very important appointment with his proctologist.

Student: What's a proctologist?

Teacher: You'll have to ask him that when he returns tomorrow.

Yes, these were childish, disgraceful, irreverent, and sometimes scary stunts. They were silly, stupid, immature, and mean, but they were done with the most affectionate of intentions, and the group of staff involved with this loved it. And this was one of the reasons, believe it or not, that made for a staff who would support each other and do anything for each other. Anyway, one of these practical jokes involved me in a roundabout way.

Our school was having our annual canned food drive in November, just in time for Thanksgiving and Christmas. The cans collected would be donated to the city's food bank. For some unknown reason, I was always fully committed to the school's canned food drive. I always gave my homeroom extra incentives to win, other than being recognized by an announcement over the school intercom. This particular year, I decided to give my students a special rationale for bringing in the most cans. I'd shave off all my hair (on my head) in front of the whole school! Now, for the average fourteen-year-old middle-schooler, this was a pretty cool incentive. It worked for all students. The students who did not particularly like me were motivated by the thought of "getting Mr. Wong." What better punishment could there possibly be for Mr. Wong other than the embarrassment of losing his hair in front of everyone? On the other hand, for those students who didn't mind me so much, this incentive was quite comical. Seeing me become instantly bald might very well be the most humorous event they have every witnessed at school. Needless to say, my homeroom won the canned food drive. And on a rainy day in December, another teacher (I'll call Mr. Zester) shaved my head on the stage connected to the school cafeteria as students were enjoying their lunch and gazing at the merriment of a teacher being humiliated.

Now, Mr. Zester was one of those teachers who willingly and enthusiastically participated in staff practical jokes. So a floor full of black and gray hair was viewed by him as having many practical joke possibilities. He wasn't sure what those might be at the time, but he knew he had some interesting contraband to ponder over. A small paper bag full of cut human hair might come in handy. And about a week later, in the staff lunchroom, I found out how.

Mr. Zester, and another teacher I'll call Mr. Hatfield, knew that our principal always kept his sack lunch in the refrigerator in the staff lounge. So during Mr. Zester's planning period, he tiptoed into the staff lounge when no one was there. He secured the principal's sack lunch and found inside a delicious tuna fish sandwich. He placed a small clump of my hair in the tuna, closed the sandwich, neatly rewrapped it, and returned it to its original location in the refrigerator. Mr. Zester then informed Mr. Hatfield of his cunning, covert act, and both eagerly anticipated lunch break on that fateful day.

When lunch arrived, the principal, Mr. Zester, and Mr. Hatfield sat down together, as usual, to replenish their bodies with some nutritious, tasty sustenance. With two sets of eyes on the principal's every move, the principal reached into his lunch sack and pulled out his neatly (re)wrapped sandwich. He unwrapped it and took his first healthy bite. To their surprise, there was no negative reaction at all from the principal as he chewed and swallowed the fishy and semihairy delight. The next bite was the same, and the next one as well! Soon, the entire sandwich was totally consumed, with nary a hint from the principal that he had just eaten a bunch of my hair. Mr. Zester and Hatfield were startled and amazed at this stupefying turn of events. The expectation was that the principal would take his first bite, notice an unsettling texture, spit it out, and discover what appeared to be human or animal hair. But he ate the whole sandwich with not a hint of anything wrong. So Mr. Zester and Hatfield left the lunchroom, a bit perplexed, and decided to inform the principal of his odd eating behavior the next day at lunch.

Mr. Zester began the exchange between himself and the principal, who was now munching on a ham-and-cheese sandwich. I'll call the principal Jack.

"Hey, Jack, how's your day going?" Mr. Zester exclaimed.

"So far, so good," responded Jack.

"I was wondering, Jack, if you happen to remember the kind of sandwich you ate for lunch yesterday."

"Yes, I do. I'm pretty sure it was tuna fish."

"Yes, that's correct," confirmed Mr. Zester, "and did you notice anything unusual about it?"

"No, I didn't," the principal remarked with a quizzical look on his face.

"Well, remember when Mr. Wong shaved his head because of the incentive he offered his students for winning the canned food drive?"

"Yes," the principal hesitantly confirmed, now clearly imagining that something was up.

"Well, I took a clump of Mr. Wong's hair and mushed it into the tuna," Mr. Zester matter-of-factly boasted as a sadistic, smug smirk began to form on his face.

Jack, who was a full-fledged member of the practical joke club at school, initially grimaced at the idea of ingesting my hair. He stuck his tongue out ever so slightly and mumbled a sound that resembled a muffled "yuk." I'm sure, up to this point in his life, eating human hair had been the grossest thing he'd ever consumed. And sometimes finding out after the fact is worse. At this moment, my hair was somewhere in his digestive system making its way home.

Within a few seconds, however, the principal was smiling and giving Mr. Zester and Hatfield high-fives. He knew there were six months left in the school year, and there would be plenty of opportunities to make Mr. Zester and Mr. Hatfield's day as wonderful as his was today.

Chapter 17

Future Teachers of America

Mother: How do you like your new teacher?

Son: I don't. He told me to sit up front for the present, and then he didn't give me one.

've had four student teachers assigned to me during my thirty-four-year career. These lucky college students were majoring in education and wanted to be full-fledged teachers in the very near future. The last task they must complete before accomplishing this goal was to apply what they had learned at the university by teaching in a real school under the mentorship of an experienced master teacher. This process usually involved a few weeks of observation, a few weeks of helping individual students, and maybe teaching a few lessons here and there. Eventually, the student teacher would take over a couple of classes and, by the end of the semester, teach all of the master teacher's classes. The master teacher, meanwhile, observed and evaluated the student teacher. He or she would also offer sound, experience-proven suggestions and recommendations.

Just like any group of human beings, student teachers came with a variety of personality quirks. One female student teacher I had could not handle misbehaving students and, in front of the class, broke down crying several times. She was so excited to present to the students the multimedia lesson she had worked on for three hours the night before. So when the students were not paying attention, she simply couldn't take it. A male student teacher I mentored rode a Harley-Davison 1200 Sportster to school, wore a long ponytail, possessed a rather bountiful beer gut, and allowed the students to use and abuse him. He had a bad habit of always allowing the students to talk even while he was trying to explain some concept. And what bothered me the most was that it didn't seem to bother him at all! But none of these came close to my most memorable student teacher, whom I will call Mr. Joe Greeley.

Usually, schools get student teachers from the local universities, which geographically makes sense. But Joe came from a college five hundred miles away. This fact alone should have raised multiple red flags. But he said he was staying with relatives in the area so, okay, that explains it.

Anyway, Joe came into my room and courteously did his couple weeks of observation. He sat quietly, occasionally and appropriately helping students, as well as asking me pertinent questions concerning the art of teaching. He was also a part-time poet and had a website revealing some of his talents, which were, by my estimation, border-line brilliant. I felt I was very lucky to have such a budding prodigy of an educator to stamp with my experience.

Mr. Joe Greeley's first endeavor in front of the class went well. He explained a literary concept—similes. Similes are comparisons between two things using *like* or *as* in between. He had students write original similes followed by presenting them to the class, and he praised and critiqued each one suitably. It was, by all accounts, a lesson befitting a veteran teacher. After the lesson, at lunch, Joe was beside himself with joy.

"I've found my calling," he passionately proclaimed. "I now know what I want to do for the rest of my life!" I couldn't have been happier for him, for my students, and for myself. I was giving the future of education an enthusiastic, proficient teacher who will, no doubt, positively impact thousands of minds during his unfaltering, distinguished career...Then things began to change.

Mr. Greeley's next task was to teach a novel called *My Brother Sam Is Dead* to my eighth grade language arts class. This book is historical fiction that tells the story of Tim, a fourteen-year-old living in Connecticut during the Revolutionary War and his conflicts with his Loyalist father and Patriot brother who decides to join the Continental Army. The novel complimented and reinforced what the eighth-graders were currently learning in their US history classes.

So Joe began his first lesson by passing out the books and asking the students to turn to page one. Just then, a student raised his hand.

"Mr. Greeley, I was wondering what you like to do for fun."

"I'm so glad you asked that question!" Mr. Greeley gleefully responded. "Just give me a second, and I'll get you your answer immediately!"

Joe then threw down the book, jumped up, and began to assemble a multimedia presentation. He pulled wires from a bag he had in the corner of the room, secured a projector from the closet, and pulled from his pocket (no joke!) a film that he then swiftly dispatched into the waiting projector. I have never seen anyone so tech savvy, so capable and fast at compiling the necessary components for a media presentation in my life! Within thirty seconds, Mr. Greeley was articulating the answer to the student's inquiry.

"See the guy in the red shirt to the left of me in this photo," Mr. Greeley excitedly avowed, "he's my best friend, and his name is Jack. We're at Yellowstone National Park. Man, that was a fun trip. You probably can't tell from this photo, but Jack is high. He just smoked some weed, and that is why he's grinning from ear to ear. He's in a really cool place in this picture. He's had drug problems in the past, but he's really making a splendid attempt to control his urges. He's a totally great friend."

"Um, Mr. Greeley, who's that lady in the picture?" voiced a wide-eyed boy in the back, whose sole purpose was to have Mr. Greeley continue with his most fascinating and edgy discourse.

"That lady is my ex-girlfriend. We're still friends. We've been through a lot together. We lived together for about a year. She thought she was freaking pregnant one time! But luckily, the pregnancy test was negative. But that's not why we broke up. I don't know, the whole breakup thing was sort of weird. But we're still warmhearted friends, and we continue to share many things together, like this trip we took."

This kind of jibber-jabber confessional by Mr. Greeley lasted the rest of the period, a good twenty-five minutes. I was sitting in the back of the classroom, listening with a mind-set of shock and nauseating engagement. I couldn't believe the improper things he was saying to impressionable middle schoolers. Would I get calls from parents complaining? Would the principal hold me responsible, or at least, partially responsible, for my student teacher's poor judgment? I had to do something about this immediately. My job could be, literally, in the balance!

So after class, I told Joe we needed to talk, "Mr. Greeley, there are a number of things you should know about eighth grade classroom etiquette and about accomplishing lesson goals," I confidently declared to Joe. "I'm sorry, but you should never use the adjective *freaking* with these kids."

"But I didn't say *fucking*, so I thought it was okay."

"No, Joe, it's not okay. And talking about drugs and pregnancy with students of this age is really inappropriate. And did you notice that you never got around to introducing the novel? So you'll have to do that first thing tomorrow. Make sure you stick to the lesson plan and not let the students sidetrack you."

Joe's face lit up a bit as if he understood everything I was telling him. "Oh, okay, Mr. Wong, and thanks. Those are some very good suggestions."

Whew! So maybe the whole incident was an innocent mistake. New, young teachers often have the misconception of trying to please students and become their friends. This, they believe, will nourish their likeability, and thus students will want to academically succeed. But the average fourteen-year-old will use, abuse, and eat these kinds of teachers alive. They may "like" the teacher at the time, similar to an audience enjoying a clown juggling foam balls. But they know it's a scam. And when they realize they haven't learned the established curriculum that is crucial to doing well the next school year, they feel ripped off and angry.

Anyway, I felt my talk with Joe made a big difference. He understood what he needed to do and realized appropriate social boundaries. He was enlightened about the importance of sticking to the lesson plan…Boy, was I wrong!

The next day, again inspired by a steering-away-from-doing-actual-schoolwork question, by a student who knew there was a gullible pushover for a teacher in charge—Mr. Greeley rattled on about his personal life and, again, never even began to introduce the novel. He did, however, offer an extra credit assignment.

"Students, on the blackboard, I've written down an extra credit assignment." Mr. Greeley smiled and proudly made his way to the back of the classroom to point out and explain his most interesting assignment. "Now, for ten extra credit points, you can write a paragraph about what you learn when you go to the bathroom. Make sure you have a topic sentence, good transitions, and clear, specific details. Oh, and no potty humor will be allowed."

I couldn't believe what I was hearing as I sat in the back, evaluating Mr. Greeley. But my astonishment and frustration gave way to a sense of relief. There was something obviously deeply wrong with Joe. And it had nothing to do with my mentoring or influence. I now realized what I needed to do. I would inform the principal. I'd explain how Mr. Greeley did not listen to my suggestions, was not following academic lesson plans, and was, at best, marginally socially appropriate. Unfortunately, I would have to confess to the principal that Mr. Greeley was simply not fit to be a teacher. The principal would then have to regrettably release Mr. Greeley from his current student teacher placement at this school, and my nightmare would be over.

To my surprise, however, the principal, never having observed Mr. Greeley himself, told me that I should let Joe continue for a while longer. After all, my negative assessment of Mr. Greeley was merely a matter of different teaching styles. I ran a pretty tight ship. When students worked on an assignment, the class was absolutely quiet. When I lectured in front of the class, the student's eyes were on me, and if they wanted to ask a question, they needed to raise their hand and wait until I called on them. I guess I was sort of like Mr. Hand in the movie *Fast Times at Ridgemont High*. So I, according to the principal, was simply coloring my evaluation of Mr. Greeley through my rigid, old-school style of teaching. I needed to loosen up and realize my perspective may be slanted and that teaching styles different from mine can be just as effective.

While the principal was telling me this, for reasons I will soon divulge, a great weight was lifted from my shoulders. I felt like I had done what I needed to do: informed my superior, and if anything happened after this, it was on the principal. So I was now going to sit back and have some fun listening to Mr. Greeley's provocative, intriguing narratives. I would, of course, continue to do my job as his mentor teacher. But I knew he wouldn't change his approach, and the students continued to run all over him.

Word got around the school about Mr. Greeley. Teachers would pop into Joe's classroom to see what he was up to and inevitably come away with a gem of a story to relate to their colleagues at lunch. There was excitement and much anticipation amongst the staff concerning Mr. Greeley's next classroom blunder.

Mr. Greeley, on the other hand, was very pleased with all these teachers visiting his classroom. In his mind, they were there because he was such an extraordinary educator. They were obviously amazed at his powerful teaching techniques and wanted to learn from him.

One of the requirements of the student teaching process is allowing the student teacher to be without the master teacher in the classroom so that he can develop on his own. On one of these days, Ms. Cocheran, a seventh grade social studies teacher, had been in Mr. Greeley's classroom to see for herself what this most unusual teacher was up to.

I was sitting in the teacher's lounge, trying to enjoy a sip of coffee, when she ran in, out of breath, and distinctly agitated. "Roger, quick, you must go up to your classroom immediately!" Ms. Cocheran blurt out with pure panic in her voice.

"Why? What's the problem?"

"Hurry! Hurry! You need to get up there right *now!*"

"Okay, I hear you, but what's going on?"

"Okay, Mr. Greeley brought his dog to school. It's a Golden Retriever puppy. He put it on the desk, and it took a dump and then fell off. I think it's injured! Hurry! *Get up there!*"

Much to the displeasure of Ms. Cocheran, I slowly got up from the comfortable lounge couch and sauntered up to my room. Ms. Cocheran was clearly perturbed at my lack of urgency. By the time I arrived, the poop had been cleaned up, with just a trace of polluted odor remaining. Mr. Greeley was holding his puppy as I addressed him, "Mr. Greeley, is your puppy injured?"

"No, it's fine."

"Well, Mr. Greeley, you need to take your puppy home right now. I'll take over the class while you are gone."

"Okay, Mr. Wong, but I was just in the middle of telling the students about the benefits of having a good-sized yard if you own a dog."

"Mr. Greeley, take your puppy home *now*, and come back as soon as you can."

"Okay, Mr. Wong," replied Joe with a mystified look on his face.

Mr. Greeley hesitantly departed with puppy in hand. (He never returned to school that day.)

A shy, fidgety, straight A student in the front raised her hand.

"Yes, Melanie, you have a question?" I asked as Mr. Greeley closed the classroom door behind him.

"Mr. Wong, does this mean we are actually going to start the novel?"

"Yes, Melanie, we are."

The next day, the principal called Mr. Greeley into his office and gave him the bad news. He would have to leave the campus immediately and, if he so desired, seek out a student teaching placement at another school.

Chapter 18

Critical Thinking

A young high school math teacher, Ms. Lambright, notices a student, Dylan, has fallen asleep in her class. As a joke, and to embarrass him a bit, she wakes him up and asks him a question:

"If three ducks were sitting on a fence, and you shoot one, how many are left?"

"None," says Dylan, "because the shot would scare the rest off."

"Well, the answer is two," replies Ms. Lambright, "but I like how you are thinking."

Dylan now has a question of his own for Ms. Lambright. "If you see three women walking out of Baskin and Robbins, and one is licking her ice cream, the second is biting her ice cream, and the third is sucking her ice cream, which one is married?"

Not quite sure how to answer, Ms. Lambright replies, "The one sucking her ice cream?"

"No," says Dylan, "the one with the wedding ring, but I like how you are thinking."

ales are perverts, and women have been forever telling us this fine fact. Even from a very young age, the thoughts of boys are crowded with sexual thoughts. They may not even know exactly how babies are made, yet their thinking is cluttered with erotic scenarios.

I remember my seventh grade social studies teacher. Oh, do I remember her! I'll call her Ms. Garver, and she was cute as a button. She was the first crush I ever had for a live, breathing, actual person I knew. I had many crushes before, but they were for fictional women in magazines or on TV. For example, I thought a lot, when I was eleven, about Ginger (Tina Louise) on *Gilligan's Island* or Samantha (Elizabeth Montgomery) on *Bewitched*. And the genie (Barbara Eden) on *I Dream of Jeannie* sent warm shivers up my leg. But Ms. Garver was real and right in front of me for an hour a day, five days a week!

I was smart enough to know that *miss* meant she wasn't married and thus available. And all I could do was gaze at her and dream. She was a good teacher as well. I have always remembered that *latitude* stood for the imaginary horizontal lines that measure the earth in degrees, because of Ms. Garver's clever mnemonic device.

"Now, class, you will always remember that latitude refers to the horizontal lines and longitude refers to the vertical lines by thinking of latitude as '*flat*itude.'" Then she smiled and sent me to heaven.

I really thought there was a good chance we would start hanging out after seventh grade. We couldn't do it *now*—that would be inappropriate; we still had to maintain the facade of student and teacher. But, boy, this summer we'll be riding our bikes, having picnics by the lake, and cozying up on the couch while watching *Get Smart* and *Leave It to Beaver*. We'd eventually get married and have some kids, even though I was unsure how having kids occurred.

Then one day, there was a knock at her classroom door. A man entered. My Ms. Garver ran to him and kissed him on the lips and gave him a big hug. I was devastated, crushed, humiliated, and hurt. My little heart felt like it had been strung up and used as a punching bag. My life's plan had dissolved right before my eyes.

I was really late in learning about sex. I grew up way before the Internet, or TV shows, like the ones today, that show just about everything. For Christ's sake, the word *pregnant* wasn't even allowed when Lucy became visibly "with child" on *I Love Lucy*. Also, the rule was, if a scene on a TV program happened to take place in a bedroom, at least one of their feet had to be touching the ground! So there was little media information that helped me figure out how babies were made, and the *Playboy* magazines I secretly secured and hid in the attic didn't help answer any serious questions I had. Also, my parents never sat me down to tell me about the birds and the bees either. I'm not sure why. I think they may have been too embarrassed. Or maybe they figured I already knew, or they assumed it was the school's responsibility.

In fact, in middle school is where I finally learned the truth about how it's done. It was toward the end of seventh grade, and all students were required to take sex education training. It was about time I learned the truth because, up until this time, I thought pregnancy occurred via a chemical reaction when kissing someone of the opposite sex.

In these days, circa 1965, they separated the boys and girls and sent each group to a different part of the school. The boys went to the cafeteria where we watched a rather clinical black-and-white movie about how a woman gets pregnant. I remember it was rather confusing. The reproductive system of a woman looked like a cow's head and those swimming sperm like tadpoles. But at the very end, they finally put it all together by saying, "Then the man will insert his penis in the woman's vagina, ejaculate, and pregnancy may occur."

Well, this shocked the hell out of me! For one, I *knew* my parents never did this, yet they must have, since I'm here, along with my two brothers and one sister. Okay, they did it four times, but that's all. Also, although I was very familiar with erections (my own only), I had a hard time conceiving a scenario where it would end up in that spot on a woman. Anyway, after that bit of knowledge was inserted into my brain, my thinking changed.

My next crush was in tenth grade. My language arts teacher, whom I will call Ms. McCoy, was young. Interestingly enough, though, she wasn't particularly pretty in her face. But the way she talked, walked, and swayed oozed with sexiness. She was one of those cool teachers who played teen music while students entered her class. When the music stopped, it meant class was starting.

Short skirts were in at this time, and Ms. McCoy always kept up with the latest fashions. I had a hard time concentrating in class because all I could do was longingly scrutinize her every skin fold, blouse crease, and ear cranny. Knee crevices, neck nuances, and shoulder delicacies were swirling around in my fifteen-year-old libidinous imagination. When she leaned against the blackboard, with chalk in hand, I wished to God I was that chalk. I was in love. I can't remember exactly how long this crush lasted, but it was a wonderful experience. For at least nine months, I was never wanton of someone to think about in the privacy of my room.

It's no secret that men have very frequent sexual thoughts. And they cannot help it. I remember in college sitting in a sociology class titled "Sociology of Sexual Behavior" and the professor telling us that adult males have a sexual thought every six seconds. What? Wow! Now that's frequent! I'm not sure how they determined that, though. I picture a graduate assistant dressed in a white lab coat, holding a clipboard and stopwatch, and asking a male college volunteer to let him know if a sexual thought enters his mind. I'll bet if that graduate assistant was a young female, frequency would rise.

Even Jimmy Carter bravely admitted he has these kinds of thoughts in a 1976 interview with *Playboy* magazine where he stated, "I've looked at a lot of women with lust. I've committed adultery in my heart many times." As you may recall, Jimmy Carter was governor of Georgia and later president of the United States. He was, and still is, considered by many to be the most kindhearted, religious-oriented politician in America.

So if you are a guy, don't beat yourself up over your frequent sexual thoughts. Don't say to yourself, "Oh, no! There I go again having sexual thoughts about the neighbor lady. What's wrong with me? Am I a certifiable sexual deviant? Do I need counseling? Has the devil taken over my soul?" No, it's none of these things. It's simply because you are a guy. You are wired differently. You cannot help it, and you have to live with this curse your entire life. Males are just helplessly and hopelessly stuck with perpetual carnal cognition. This is an enigmatic dilemma that cannot be easily turned off, whether you are eating at McDonald's, sitting at home watching TV, or at school.

Anyway, I always wondered if any student (male or female) ever had a crush on me during my teaching career. For the life of me, I cannot imagine why they would have. Did my portly belly flab hanging over my belt turn them on? Maybe they liked the swishing sound of my tight slacks as they rubbed against my inner thighs when I walked to the other side of the room for a dictionary. Or could it be my pudgy cheeks (on my face) that they imagined stroking? Maybe the strength in my voice when I said, "Sit down. Shut up. Get to work," caused them to dream about a life with someone who would protect them and provide for them…Nah! Anyway, if there ever was a student who had a crush on me, I'll never know for sure.

I did have a few ambiguous conversations with senior girls, though. But my social radar never allowed me to believe they were actually coming on to me. And they probably weren't. They were just super nice kids, friendly, charming, and unknowingly sexy.

> Female student: Hi, Mr. Wong! I really love that shirt you have on today.
> Me: Well, thanks, Bridgette. I think I got this shirt at Sears.
> Bridgette: Really? I *love* shopping at Sears. I can never find a ride there, though. When is the next time you are going?
> Me: Huh…Um…I'm not sure.
> Bridgette: Well, let me know the next time you go so I can ride down with you, especially if it's over the weekend. [A big smile crosses her face, and I thought I detected some eye fluttering.)

And…

> Me: Rebecca, I don't think you fully understand the criteria for this five-paragraph paper. Do you need some extra help?

Rebecca: Yes, I think I do. But I'm so busy after school. I'm on the school's gymnastics team and also practice at a gym downtown to improve.

Me: Wow, you are busy.

Rebecca: Yes, but I love gymnastics. Have you ever seen a gymnastics meet, Mr. Wong? You should come to my next meet. It's this Friday night. We just got new gymnastics tights too. They are blue around here. [She takes her finger and runs it slowly from her shoulder down the side of her right breast.] And then there is gold striping in this area. [She places her hand gently on her lower stomach, dangerously close to her you-know-what.] And the bottom part is solid red. [She delicately moves her hand from her lower stomach to her actual you-know-what.]

She then abruptly looked up at me and caught me admiring her you-know-what. I was startled and embarrassed. But she broadly smiled, as if to say, "That's okay, Mr. Wong, *you* may look and enjoy."

Me: Well, Rebecca, those new tights sound very beautiful.

Rebecca: Yes, but you really need to see them in person to know how beautiful they actually are. Will you come to my meet this Friday?

Me: Well, I'll have to check my calendar and see what my *wife* is doing. Thanks for the invitation, though... now, what were we talking about?

Chapter 19

Airheads

Little Billy was sitting on a park bench, munching on one candy bar after another. After the sixth one a man sat on the bench across from him and said:

"Son, you know, eating all that candy isn't good for you. It will give you acne, rot your teeth, and make you fat."

Little Billy replied, "Well, you know, my grandfather lived to be 107 years old!'

"Oh," replied the man, "did your grandfather eat six candy bars at a time?"

"No," replied Little Billy, "he minded his own fucking business!"

Kids love candy. You've all been told, by your parents growing up, to never take candy from a stranger. And why would you, unless you loved candy! Just as a perverted stranger might offer a kid candy to lure him or her into his van, many teachers use candy as an incentive for students to behave or try harder on their assignments. Okay, I guess that was an inappropriate, unpleasant comparison, but I think you get the point I'm trying to make. Candy works.

Now some of you may think that using candy in the classroom is wrong. Shouldn't teachers be instilling in their students the value of intrinsic rewards? Students should behave and try hard because they know it's the right way to be, that self-assessment of one's conduct as a human being is enough to aspire a kid to greatness. A student should not expect a tangible reward for simply acting the way they ought to act in class. He ought to know, deep down, it's the proper way to carry oneself and experience the inner joy when doing so. Inner dialogue, such as, "I'm a moral, cooperative, good person," or "I'm behaving honorably and making the world a better place," will keep the student on the right track...Well, *bullshit!*

People who believe that intrinsic rewards, by themselves, work as an incentive probably aren't teachers...or parents, or day care workers, or belong to any profession or life position where children are present. Now, I'm not saying teachers should ignore informing students of the value of intrinsic rewards. They really should. But this kind of worthy information is usually not part of a teacher's required curriculum. Today's teachers simply do not have time for such a worthwhile academic endeavor. And it doesn't work as well as candy, anyway.

Yes, candy works better and faster. A kid who throws a book across the room and acts out frequently needs to stop *now* for the safety and sake of the other students. The teacher cannot stop the lesson, take him aside, and explain to him how much better he would feel about himself if he hadn't done that. First, the student wouldn't buy it and think you were the king of the nerds. And second, meanwhile, the other kids would be texting on their phones messages to each other about what an idiot the teacher is even though they appreciate the time to be on their cell phones.

Yet if that misbehaving student *knew* he wouldn't get any candy at the end of the class period if he did something like throw a book, he very well may not have tossed it to begin with. In other words, I have found that concrete compensation for behaving, or doing well in class, works quickly, effectively, and even as a preventative measure in many cases. I have found this to be true for elementary and middle school kids especially, but even the eyes of high school kids light up when they hear that candy may be at stake. And at the middle school I taught at, a new school policy was started where the power of candy would be tested.

It was around my fifteenth year of teaching middle school when a new "incentive" program was initiated one fine year called "positive behavior support," or PBS for short. *All* teachers were required to use it—no matter what effective, or ineffective, classroom management techniques they had displayed previously. This was a schoolwide, we-need-to-stick-together-as-teachers approach. Like many new school policies at this particular school, a small group of teachers and administrators had formed a committee and made this decision over the summer. Usually, I detest these fly-by-night decisions. It just seemed to me, the proper way to kick off a new policy that affects everyone is to get some staff input first, and maybe have a vote, in order to get maximum staff buy in.

So as I was patiently listening to the explanation and inevitable enactment of this new PBS program at the September faculty meeting, I was naturally skeptical and doubtful it would work, especially since I rarely had any major classroom management issues. But as I let the specifics of the program penetrate my thinking, I concluded it might actually have some value.

Basically, PBS involved giving premade paper PBS slips to students for good behavior, absence of bad behavior, better-than-average effort, or exceptional academic performance. In turn, these slips would be collected by the student and turned in for various rewards. The school offered rewards like one slip for one small piece of hard candy, five slips for moving to the front of the lunch line, and ten slips for eating lunch with a teacher of your choice.

The school rewards, in my opinion, were well intentioned, but rather lame. For example, I couldn't think of too many teachers who wanted to have lunch with a student. They needed the time to grade papers, get ready for the next class, or wind down from the morning classes. It was impossible to do this while making small talk with a thirteen-year-old who thinks you actually want to be there. And

I didn't know too many students who wanted to eat lunch with a teacher. After all, lunch was their only "teacher free" time all day. And what thirteen-year-old would rather be talking shop with a teacher over digesting juicy gossip with their friends? Let's be real here!

Fortunately, the PBS system allowed individual teachers to offer other favors to their students for PBS slips, at their own expense, of course. Thank goodness. Enter in my classroom *Airheads*, the candy.

With the power of candy and the thought of out-of-pocket expenditures looming in my mind, I found myself at Sam's Club, hoping to find some extremely cheap, yet teen-approved confectionery. Ah, yes! Airheads! I could get a whole box of Airhead candies, consisting of ninety bars, for $9.00. I'm not a math teacher, but I believe that works out to be ten cents per bar. Score! What a deal! So I bought two boxes, brought them to my classroom, and wrote on my whiteboard the fact that for every two PBS slips earned, you would be the proud owner of an Airhead.

Now, in my classroom, you could earn PBS slips for a myriad of behaviors. An excellently organized or expertly executed assignment may get you slips. Slips may be handed to you for no tardies during the month or no off-task points during the week. PBS slips might be stapled to your test for an exceptional score or given to you for remembering to bring your book to class. I purposely made it somewhat easy to get slips. All you had to do was behave, be organized, and be polite. And if you wanted some gravy on your mashed potatoes, earn high marks for even more slips.

And I noticed something curious right off the hat. The students really wanted Airheads! The school rewards for slips were a mere distraction, a back-of-the-mind kind of diversion. My students desperately desired these candies. I didn't keep strict records, but it seemed to me that the vast majority of the slips I gave to students were returned to me for Airheads.

There're probably some of you reading this who are not quite sure exactly what Airheads are or why a middle schooler might want them so much. Well, Airheads are taffy-like bars, individually wrapped, and are approximately four by one inches in size. They are chewy, if you choose to chew them. Many like to snip off a bit and let it slowly dissolve on the tongue like a heavenly version of cotton candy. Unlike cotton candy, however, the bit of Airhead will last for many marvelous minutes, like an intravenous drip delivering a constant, exquisite sugar high. They come in a variety of flavors, including grape, cherry, orange, watermelon, blue raspberry, and the risk-taking, danger-enhanced "white mystery" flavor. After talking with students, however, apparently, "white mystery" is simply one of the other flavors, colored white by some cancer-causing, sugar-energized, unhealthy additive. All I know is that my middle school students *loved* Airheads!

So the behavior and academic achievement of my students actually improved, thanks to the new PBS system and my offering of Airheads for PBS slips. Yet there were a few students who very much wanted Airheads but never had any slips. These students were nice enough folks but were always on the outskirts of earning a coveted PBS slip. Many of the students felt sorry for these students who couldn't cash in on an Airhead. Anyway, one of these students, whom I will call Jake, approached me one day with a sincere, straightforward question.

"Mr. Wong, I don't have any PBS slips, as you probably know, but I was wondering if I could possibly *buy* an Airhead?"

I had never thought about students buying Airheads from me. It had never crossed my mind, so I wasn't quite sure how to respond. "Um, well, Jake, I'm not sure about that. The Airheads are basically reserved for those who have earned slips."

"I know, Mr. Wong, but I didn't eat any breakfast this morning. And quite frankly, I'm *starving.*"

Now, as a teacher, when you hear a statement like this, many thoughts begin swirling around in your brain. Was he *starving* in the sense of him purposely or accidentally skipping breakfast, thus finding himself in this unique conundrum? Or was he telling me, in a semicryptic manner, that he was being neglected and abused at home? Were his parents not feeding him and I was now in a position to help him survive the day? If I questioned him about his parents or possible neglect, it could be perceived as intrusive and personally embarrassing.

So in an attempt to do the right thing, save face for the student, and help a destitute child, I heard myself responding, "Okay, Jake, I guess I could sell you an Airhead. I'm not sure how much I should ask, though. Would twenty-five cents be okay with you?"

Without any hesitation whatsoever, Jake quickly replied, "Great, I'll take a dollar's worth." As I handed over four Airheads, he became instantly giddy, and I thought I detected some Pavlovian saliva dripping from his lips.

Then, within ten minutes, an unexpected thing happened. Another student without slips approached me to buy Airheads. I'll call him Nathan.

"Hey, Mr. Wong, I'd like to buy two Airheads. Here's fifty cents."

"Huh, Nathan, I don't know about this. Airheads are supposed to be for students with PBS slips."

"I know, Mr. Wong, but Jake didn't have any slips, and *you* let him buy Airheads. Why can't I?"

Now, at this juncture, I was thinking about my educational training and experience and how "consistency" is so important to the success of running a classroom. In order for a teacher to be fair to all students and respected by all, he must be consistent in administering classroom rules, positive and negative consequences, and other classroom policies. I felt I had no choice.

I already let Jake buy Airheads and broken the mold, so to speak. What could I say to Nathan that would be fair?

"No, Nathan, *you* cannot buy Airheads like Jake. You are different. Your reasons for wanting the Airheads are not as compelling. Come back when you can convince me you may be starving." *I think not!*

So with much hesitation and reservation, I told Nathan, "Okay, Nathan, you can buy a couple of Airheads."

"Thanks, Mr. Wong!" Nathan gleefully responded as I collected his fifty cents and handed him his requested grape and "white mystery" Airheads.

And so ensued an avalanche of students wanting, or *needing*, to buy Airheads—not only from my classes, but from other classes as well. They'd hurry into my room during passing time with quarters in order to score a few Airheads. I felt like an unglorified drug dealer. I had the goods, and I had a monopoly on the market. I was, quite frankly, running a nice, tidy business catering to the economic law of supply and demand.

Deep down, however, I suspected there was something not quite right about it. But I rationalized the whole thing by the fact that I used almost all of my profits from this endeavor to cover the cost of those Airheads I was purchasing with my own money and giving to students who had PBS slips.

Then one day, a student, whom I will call Robbie, came to me with a rather unusual request, "Mr. Wong, could I buy a whole box of Airheads from you?"

"What? A whole box? Robbie, that's ninety Airheads. What are you going to do with ninety Airheads?"

"Oh, I don't know. Give them to my friends. People like Airheads, you know."

"Gee whiz, Robbie, ninety Airheads at twenty-five cents each would come to…let me get my calculator…$22.50! I guess I never set any kind of policy about how many Airheads you could buy, so you got me on a technicality, Robbie. If you are sure you are going to be generous with them, I'll let you have the box for $15.00." (This was still $6.00 more than the box cost me.)

"Great, Mr. Wong. I'll take it."

So I handed him a brand-new, never-been-opened Sam's Club box of Airheads. In the back of my mind, however, I had a bad feeling about this little exchange, and about two weeks later, I found out why.

The principal called me into his office one rainy February day two weeks later. He told me that a parent had called him and wanted to know if I had sold his son a whole box of Airheads.

"Mr. Wong, did you sell Robbie Daltry a whole box of Airheads for $15.00?" my principal humbly began.

"Well…yes…I did. I'm selling Airheads to students to cover the cost of the Airheads I give away to students for earning PBS slips. The kids love them, and Robbie said he wanted that many to share with his friends."

"Actually, Mr. Wong, a lunchroom attendant caught Robbie selling them to students at lunch for thirty cents each. He was doing quite a brisk business since he was undercutting our school store cost of thirty-five cents per Airhead. He's quite the entrepreneur. I guess he got the idea from you and had been saving up his lunch money to buy Airheads from you and then selling them at a handsome profit. His parents are upset he used his lunch money for this, and rightly so."

"Oops…I had no idea."

"Mr. Wong, it's against school policies for you to sell *anything* to students. Ignorance of this policy is no excuse. Let me tell you something, I once knew a teacher who was doing this kind of thing, and before he was caught, he had made thousands of dollars. I was pressured by the district to fire him, which I did. I don't want this to happen to you. You must immediately stop selling Airheads, or I will have to take appropriate action."

"I hear you loud and clear. I'm done selling Airheads. You can bet on that." I slinked out of his office, head down, ashamed, disgraced, and determined to never set my eyes or hands on another evil Airhead.

Students didn't take the news very well. Some even argued with me, saying I was a liar and what I said couldn't be trusted. I felt bad, for maybe a minute, and then settled into thinking the chances of me being fired had been reduced significantly.

Chapter 20

Lunchtime Delight

In ninth grade language arts class, Ms. Johnson wrote on the board, "I ain't had no fun this summer." She then asked the class how this can be corrected.

A girl raises her hand and replies, "Get a boyfriend."

There was a very strict, no-tolerance rule at my middle school about public display of affection among the students. And the teachers enforced it. After all, these were eleven- to fourteen-year-olds. Kissing and holding hands were quickly corrected. Hugging another student was okay as long as it was very brief. Any "prolonged" hugs were unacceptable, and we teachers had the privilege of deciding what "prolonged" meant. Touching was allowed only at the discretion of the teacher. If a student placed her hand briefly on another student's forearm, it might be okay. But any touching anywhere near the breasts, butt, crotch, or groin may get you a ticket to the principal's office.

When I taught at a high school, however, it was a different story. These fifteen- to eighteen-year-olds were consumed with the opposite sex. It was impossible to enforce middle school–type rules.

You, as a teacher, would have to spend your entire day trying to get students to stop touching each other, and it just wouldn't be worth it. Nothing else would get done. So it was very common to walk down the halls and see, within a span of one hundred feet, several students holding hands, several others with their arms around each other, and maybe one or two couples kissing or making out. During my first few years, I'd try to intervene, thinking it was the proper thing to do. I mean, if visitors to the school saw this, they may think our mission statement was way too promiscuous.

I always felt a little uncomfortable when approaching two students making out in the hallway. The conversation usually caused me to feel really old and like a jerk.

> Me: Huh, could you two please stop?
> Male student: Stop what, Mr. Wong?
> Me: Well, stop what you are doing.
> Female student: We're not doing anything wrong or illegal, are we?
> Me: Huh, I guess not, but I think it's inappropriate, so I'm asking you to stop.
> Male student: Okay, we'll stop, but I think you forgot what it was like to be young, Mr. Wong. C'mon, Sandra, let's get out of here.

So after a few years, I simply pretended like I didn't see them. I'd coincidentally turn my head when I passed them, acting like I just saw something on the opposite wall that drew my attention away. Some teachers, on the other hand, would stroll right up to them, stand within arm's reach, say nothing, and stare. To me, this was like accidentally catching your best friend and his wife, butt naked, on your couch after all the other partygoers had departed for home. The students, however, would get the message. They'd temporarily stop, only to move to a more private area of the school.

To be true, touching in a sexual manner was never compatible with the ideals of "school." Schools were places where your mind should grow, not other things. Schools focused on cerebral pursuits, not running after that cutie from second period social studies class.

Schools were supposed to increase your intellectual potential, not your lustful cravings. But sometimes, even teachers caved in to these sensual desires while at school. And for a couple of months, I found myself to be like some out-of-control, horny, insatiable student.

My classroom, during lunch period, became aghast with two people passionately making out, hugging, and touching each other semi-inappropriately. One of those people was a newly hired thirty-nine-year-old special education teacher. And the other person was me.

My first wife divorced me in 2002, after twenty-two years of marriage and two kids. It wasn't a particularly bitter divorce, but I was quite angered and devastated over the breakup of the family unit and only being able to see my fourteen- and nine-year-old daughters every other week.

During these months, I'd find myself, during a video or quiet work period, with my head down, staring at the floor. My shoulders and back would be slumped, and I was numb with emotional anguish. A student could have got up and walked right out the door, and I probably would not have noticed. The students probably thought I was tired or getting too old to carry myself normally or deep in thought about the pop quiz I was going to give them at the end of the period. This was during my twenty-third year of teaching. I was fifty years old and a bit out of shape.

After my long hiatus from dating, I was totally terrified and intimidated about returning to the dating scene. I realized I had actually forgotten how to date! And the dating world was much different today compared to twenty-two years ago. Back then, there were no personal computers, gas was $1.50 per gallon, and the women's liberation movement was in its infancy. Furthermore, when I looked in the mirror, extra pounds were staring back at me, not to mention the gray that was secretly invading my heretofore beautiful black hair. But at least I still had a full head of hair! Yes, I was ahead of the dating game on this physical point compared to many other fifty-year-olds! With much energy and effort, I tried to gather inside of me self-confidence, a productive attitude, and a deliberate conviction because, deep in my soul, the whole dating thing scared the living shit out of me!

What the hell am I supposed to do or not do? Should I assume I will be paying, since I'm the man and that's the gentlemanly thing to do? Or will the women see that as a slam to her financial prowess? Should I join a computer dating service to save time, or will that just let every weirdo, wigged-out, wacky woman have access to my sincere and sacrificing personality? Do I make the first move physically, or does she? How can I tell if she wants me to make a move? Fluttering eyes? Open body language? How can I tell the difference between her simply liking me, and *liking* me? As you can see, I was one messed up fifty-year-old, trying to figure out the current dating rules and regulations.

All of my teacher "friends," of course, were trying their best to look out for me, encouraging me to find another soul mate. One woman teacher friend told me that I really must find someone pretty soon since there's nothing worse than dying "alone." I guess she thought these would be uplifting, inspiring words of wisdom. If she wasn't such a good friend, I would have responded by letting her know that, unless the husband and wife die simultaneously, like in a plane or car crash, one of them will be dying "alone" anyway. But people kept trying to set me up with dates, so I decided I might as well try one or two.

My first prearranged date was with a very good-looking woman in her early forties. We decided to meet at a bar (red flag!), and I can remember saying to myself, upon first seeing her walk through the tavern door, "All right! Come to your daddy!"

We sat down, ordered a drink, and began some pleasant, yet inane conversation. I couldn't help but stare at this middle-aged beauty. For a forty-something woman, she was very attractive, indeed. Her shoulder-length blond hair, fit physique, enchanting blue eyes, and warmhearted smile all confirmed to me she was a keeper.

Then she pulled out a cigarette and lit it.

Okay, fine, I thought. Even though I wasn't a smoker myself, I could handle a girlfriend who smoked a bit, especially if she was as pleasing to the eyes as I so enthusiastically detailed above. But as soon as her first cigarette was extinguished, she immediately lit another one. And as soon as that one was smoked, she lit yet another one. She was evidently a chain smoker, or could it be that she was extremely nervous being around such a great guy as myself?

No, she was a chain smoker. It was around the tenth cigarette, about an hour into the evening, that I began coughing from the sheer volume and thickness of the side stream smoke surrounding me. I remember her asking me, in the most polite manner, whether her smoking was bothering me. Trying to mask my lack of oxygen and sore, itchy throat, I respectfully and tactfully replied in the negative. No problem, I haven't really noticed the smoke at all! Needless to say, her incessant smoking, along with her detailed descriptions of her issues with diabetes, along with a few other medical conditions, made her outward physicality unappealing. And we never saw each other again.

It didn't take long for word of my divorce to make its way around the school. And a funny, unexpected thing happened. I discovered a few female staff members now had designs on me! One of these women started e-mailing me with subtle, yet consistent messages of how sorry she feels over my divorce and wanted to know if she could do anything to make things better. She brought me fresh-baked bread one day and seemed to coincidentally always be around. I thought nothing of it, since she was already married, and I absolutely had no interest in her. To put it quite bluntly, I was not physically attracted to her, which unfortunately is important to men, and many women as well, if they would only admit it. At one time, twenty years ago, I'm sure her husband was quite captivated by her physical charms, but Father Time hadn't been very kind to her. And to make matters worse, another staff member had, as a joke, confided to her that I liked her. This was a fiendish absurdity, indeed, but one that was enough for her to want to divorce her husband in order to be with me. It took some clever avoidance, well-timed fabrication, and fine-tuned finagling to finally get out of this one.

I taught at a middle school at the time of my divorce, and there's an old saying in the teaching profession that "You *are* what you teach." I guess there's some truth to this since there were two other female staff members who, upon hearing of my divorce, decided to take the middle school approach to the situation.

One day, a good friend of mine approached me with a sly grin and said, "Hey, Roger, how are you doing?"

"Fine, what's up?"

"Well, I was wondering if you had thought about going a little different direction in your search for a mate. I'm just asking, you know."

"What do you mean?"

"Well, have you ever thought about Ms. Vilner? I mean, thought of her as a possible date?"

"No, my God, no."

"Okay, I'm just asking. No problem."

Then it hit me. Obviously, Ms. Vilner had inquired about me and had asked my friend to, in essence, ask me if I liked her. This is what happens in a middle school lunchroom on a daily basis. Suzy's best friend, upon Suzy's request, will go and ask John, the starting center on the basketball team, if he likes Suzy. If the answer is "no," then a lot of unnecessary social bullshit is prevented. If "yes," then Suzy can proceed in the hunt for John. Looking at it this way, maybe the middle school method isn't so bad after all.

On another occasion, the same friend came to me with another very subtle inquiry about if I had ever thought about a particular staff member. In this case, though, it was concerning the female vice principal of the school. Now, this was semidangerous ground since I was a lowly teacher and she was the VP, my immediate boss. The general rule was that fraternization like this would be frowned upon and could cause major problems. I wasn't interested anyway. So any possible internal trouble was easily avoided.

Nevertheless, I was taken aback, in an odd, but admirable way, at the prospect of having female staff members wanting to connect with me. I hadn't had the slightest idea that I had been on their minds at all. It was, at the same time, both refreshing and creepy.

Anyway, about two years after my divorce, I was tired of the dating crap. There were too many weirdos out there, females with way too much baggage, hang-ups, and issues. I simply decided I was going to be okay with never hooking up again. I'd just be a happy bachelor, going about the business of enjoying life as much as I could, not worrying about if I had another human being to share my life with. Quite frankly, a great weight was lifted from my shoulders as I proceeded forward without the intense pressure to find someone. Anyway, this was my approach until a new special education teacher was hired at my school.

It was the beginning of the school year, at the staff retreat, where I first saw her. I was smitten by her long brown hair and angelic features. Although she denies it to this day, she could have been Maria Shriver's twin sister, a Maria Shriver at age thirty-nine. I was determined to get to know her that very day. And this would be easier and much more convenient since she now was working at the same school.

At the end of the business part of the retreat, where we discussed class loads, students, extracurricular activities, and the like, those who wanted to could stay and, in essence, enjoy food, drink, and general merriment. Fortunately, she stayed. This allowed me the opportunity to happen upon her and maybe get to know her. So with a revitalized approach to finding someone out there, I approached her as she was sitting on the edge of the hot tub, with her cute little feet warming in the swirling water.

We struck up a conversation, and unfortunately, I found out she was married. But for some unknown reason, I sensed something was amiss, so I offhandedly asked her if she was happy in her marriage. She immediately tilted her head downward and responded with a silence that spoke volumes. Her body language came through loud and clear.

So we immediately started seeing each other. Her immediate plans were to divorce her husband anyway. It was a done deal. I guess, technically, I was cheating, which sort of bothered me at the time, since my ex-wife had done the same thing to me. But from the very start, we were like teenage lovers, engrossed with each other's every word, absorbed with each other's interests, and making out every chance we got. I hadn't felt that exuberant in many, many years.

As I mentioned, she taught special education, and as luck would have it, her classroom was directly below mine. One simple flight of stairs was the only obstacle that separated us, and those stairs became well worn. At the beginning of every lunch period, she'd race up the stairs and scuttle into my room. I'd quickly lock the door, and we'd position ourselves leaning against the classroom sink, just out of the range of vision of anyone who happened to peer through the window slit of my door. We had, maybe, twenty minutes together at lunchtime to let our robust and renewed libidinous nature express itself. Food was the farthest thing from our minds. Now, I'm not talking about full-blown sex here. C'mon, give me some credit here! That would not be prudent at lunch, in the middle of the school day, in a public school classroom. What I'm talking about is some serious making out. I'm sure you all can relate here. Our mind-set was one of two infatuated fifteen-year-olds first giving each other permission to touch each other from the shoulders on up. Once permission is given, the devouring begins. Yes, we couldn't get enough of each other in those heavenly twenty minutes. Nonstop moans and groans gave credence to our complete and impassioned melding. Every inch of her forehead, eyes, nose, checks, mouth, teeth, gums, and neck were well known to my wanton lips and tongue. Discovering new crevices in her ears, chin, and shoulders was my favorite lunchtime pastime. You could say we successfully sucked each other's faces completely and ravenously for a couple of months. I don't think I can remember a lunchtime any more delightful than these.

You may recall, as a student at your elementary, middle, or high school, certain teachers who were noticeably different one fine day. They suddenly strutted about with a bountiful smile and exhilarating skip to their step. Their mood was elevated for some unknown reason. It may not have made sense to you why they were so giddy, so delighted to be in a classroom of students who really didn't want to be there. Maybe the teacher was sincerely trying to be positive, to make a difference in your life. Maybe they were idealistic and excited about the prospect of making their mark on the future of America.

Maybe they were on a mission to make society a better place and, in their own minds, ecstatic about improving the world through your education…or just maybe, they were making out with another teacher at lunch.

And furthermore, maybe, just maybe, those two teachers ended up getting married. Anyway, that's what happened to me.

Chapter 21

Student Discipline: Oops, Off Task!

Teacher to misbehaving student: For your punishment, write a hundred times "I will not waste my time on meaningless tasks".

During my very first week of teaching, in 1979, I happened to be visiting a colleague's classroom and standing next to his closet door. He asked me to open it up and hand him some poster paper. As I opened the door and began searching for his requested item, I noticed a paddle resting vertically just inside the door. It was about three feet long, with a handle grip and holes located on the rectangular section meant to strike the student's behind. A bit taken aback at this disconcerting discovery, I asked my colleague what this was all about.

"Hey, Thomas, what is this doing in here?" I asked while holding it up by the grip like a slimy, smelly fish.

"Oh, that's right, Roger. I forgot that this is your first year here. The school district just passed a new policy effective this year. We cannot paddle our students anymore."

"You mean," I responded halfway stunned, "that last year, and every year before that, you, as a teacher, could paddle students for misbehaving?"

"Yup," my colleague calmly retorted.

Still uncomfortable about the topic but curious as hell, I continued by asking him another question, or two. "Did you, and you alone, get to decide if a student ought to be paddled? And did you do the actual paddling?"

"Yup, and yup."

"Wow, that's hard for me to digest since I thought that was something that only occurred back in the early 1900s...or in the Deep South."

"Well, truth be told, I've paddled my share of students in the past," Thomas sheepishly admittted, "but I agree with the new policy. I think some of the older teachers, though, will miss it."

So during my first year of teaching, one method of disciplining students was no longer available to teachers in the district. I actually felt good about it and very much relieved. If I had been issued a paddle by the principal at new teacher orientation the week before, I might have asked some dumb questions, like, "What am I supposed to do with this, swat giant flies that get into the classroom? Use it to pry open my door when it gets jammed? Use it to fan myself on hot days? Could I expand the holes a bit and use it as part of a classroom climbing wall?" I don't think the principal would have appreciated my moronic comments or my twisted crack at humor.

Anyway, disciplining students has always been a "touchy" subject, yet, quite frankly, I've never been allowed to "touch" the students in any way as part of the disciplining process. In my opinion, this is an admirable approach. I believe it's not necessary to hit, slap, shake, kick, or paddle a student in order to get him or her to behave. This attitude I have is probably a result of my own upbringing. I can't remember ever being spanked by my parents or having been the recipient of any type of corporal punishment. Naturally, I never spanked my own children. I do remember one incident, however, where my rebellious teenage daughter told me to go do something to myself that was reserved only for my wife. I reacted by grabbing her shoulders and shoving her up against the nearest solid object, which happened to be the refrigerator. I then looked her in the eye and firmly conveyed to her that that comment was totally uncalled for. She subsequently left the house to cool off. But that's the closest I ever got to anything that might be viewed as corporal punishment, and that happened once during the entire time I raised my kids. Mostly, I tried to use humor, child psychology, and rewards as methods to get my two daughters to behave. And I might add that my daughters turned out splendidly as adults.

Now, having said this, I know of others who have been at the end of many a whacks. A friend of mine, who is currently a successful administrator at a nearby school district, told me that he has been "beaten" many times as a child with a switch. In case you have never heard of such a thing, a switch is a tree branch, the size of which rests somewhere between a tree limb and a tree twig. My friend remembers, when he got in trouble as a child, he'd have the privilege of selecting the switch himself. And if it wasn't of satisfactory size in the eyes of the spanker, he'd have to go back in the yard and try again, thus intensifying the inescapable nightmare. Yet my friend turned out fine. In my opinion, as long as you discipline your kids with the underlying foundation of sincere love, you're probably doing the right thing, whether you use physical punishment or not. Nevertheless, I grew up without hitting or being hit, and that's my comfort zone.

So how are teachers supposed to effectively and consistently get their students to behave? Well, about halfway through my career, a "new" technique was formulated, supposedly tested, and then became available to all teachers across the nation. It was called "Love and Logic," and many seminars, staff meetings, and credited classes were presented as the definitive answer as to how to control your incorrigible charges.

"Love and Logic" is based upon a few simple principles. First, get to know your students, and build a relationship with them. If you do this, they'll behave more like a nephew will while in the company of a respected uncle. Second, let them know you understand their problems and that you empathize with their classroom dilemmas.

And last, make sure they know that it deeply hurts and depresses you when you are required to give them negative consequences. All of these particulars can be achieved by some very simple comments to the student.

For example, the empathy part of the equation can be accomplished by responding to student complaints and concerns with comments like, "That is sooo sad," or "That must be really tough for you," or "Bummer!"

Second, developing a relationship with your students can be accomplished with what they referred to as, "I noticed..." statements. These can take the form of unpretentious comments, like, "I noticed your shoes really match your shirt today," or "I noticed you smile when I ask for volunteers to write on the board," or "I noticed you write really fast when writing in your journal." All of these "I noticed..." statements end up meaning, to the student, "I care about you and am interested in what you are doing."

And finally, to get across the point that it hurts you to give them consequences, you should say things like, "Oh, no! You're tardy again, and I'll have to give you a detention. What a bummer!" or "Oh my God, this is terrible! You were talking when I needed everyone's attention, and now I'll have to move you up front. I feel absolutely awful!" or "Dang, Jimmy, your eyes are closed. What a total bummer!" Unfortunately, I could never use this last expression because I often had students in my class with *Dang* as a last name. So if I were to use it, I might have one student I'm directing the comment to and another who is innocent and confused.

When you think about it, this whole love-and-logic technique was just using nice, comforting, nonthreatening words to get the students to sit down, shut up, and get to work. And for the most part, it was pretty effective.

When learning about this unique form of discipline, I realized I had unknowingly been doing this all along. Somehow, over the years, I had figured out that these kinds of comments work for most students and work for me. My most common empathetic phrase was, "Oh, no! Oops! You're off task!" or a close facsimile. I'd vary the words a bit, so as not to sound repetitive, but the *oops* and *off task* words were always there.

For example, I might see a student talking while I'm addressing the class, and I'd say, "Oops! You're off task! What a bummer!" Or I might see a student writing, even though I just gave them instructions to put their pens and pencils down, and I'd say, "Oops, off task, you are writing!" Or I might see a student sitting in their seat doing nothing except staring out the window, and I might say, "Oops! You're off task, you need to refocus!"

One of the stipulations when saying these empathetic statements is you need to make sure you deliver them in a genuine manner. This means it must sound sincere, like you really, really mean it, and you're hurting inside as a result. The problem, however, is that I have never been a very good actor, and so I may have deviated a bit from the "Love and Logic" rules. I think it came out a bit too over-dramatic, with a splash of irony and a hint of sarcasm. The students didn't seem to mind, though, and it worked nonetheless. I guess the students, who were a bit more cognizant concerning body language and verbal cues, noticed the sarcasm and thought it was sort of ludicrous in a semifunny kind of way. All others thought it was for real. Either way, it resulted in my kids behaving, for the most part.

So over the course of the school year, I guess the sheer number of times "Oops, off task" came out of my mouth was enormous. And this little catchphrase became synonymous with Mr. Wong. But it seemed to work for me, and I had fewer discipline problems than other teachers. So I was quite happy. Yet it hadn't crossed my mind that this little saying might actually have a negative impact on my daughters.

I have two wonderful, college-educated daughters. One of my daughters majored in Criminal Justice and ended up working at a juvenile facility as a correctional officer. She later attended a police academy and is currently working as a police officer in a small town. My other daughter majored in elementary education. She is now teaching at an elementary school in California. I'd like to believe that she decided to follow in her old man's footsteps, but that might be a bit too presumptuous.

Anyway, both my daughters attended the middle school where I taught. They never had me as a teacher personally, but many of their friends had the pleasure of my company and were thus exposed to my continual and innumerable "Oops, off task" phrase. I guess I said this at least once every class period. And if the class was particularly restless that day, I might have to say it many, many times, sort of like a nauseating broken record. It was so constant, so ceaseless and everlasting that the expression became equivalent to Mr. Wong. In mathematical language, "Oops, off task" equals Mr. Wong. To my students, "Oops, off task" and Mr. Wong were interchangeable and identical. The two things were one, like two human souls melding or merging together. One could not live without the other. One standing alone would not be recognizable. Maybe I'm exaggerating a bit. Yet according to my daughters, I'm apparently not.

When you are in middle school, you are twelve- to fourteen years old. These delicate years are characterized by many things, one of which is the belief that your parents are dumb. You clearly know more than they do. For Christ's sake, they don't even know the name of the lead singer of One Direction! Furthermore, parents are completely out of touch with the reality, the life, and the world of a fourteen-year-old. Also, the parents' sole purpose in life is to cater to your needs, but *only* when asked. Unsolicited parental help is criminal and will surely be punished with angry outbursts, such as, "*I knew that!* I'm *not* stupid, Dad," or a heavy dose of eye-rolling and/or the dreaded silent treatment lasting as long as the next time they need something. Parents are an embarrassment, and any excuse to divorce yourself from a perceived relationship with the parent is greeted with giddy acceptance. Friends' parents seem to be pretty cool. But, OMG, your parents suck!

So as my daughters were making their way through the middle school maze, occasionally (and sometimes frequently), they'd hear from their friends the horrendous saying, "Oops, off task." Now, they weren't saying it because they were doing something they weren't supposed to be doing. They were saying this to tease them about me. Basically, that short three-word term meant, "You're dad's an idiot, all he says in class is 'Oops, off task.'" So with the middle school mind-set being what it was, my daughters suffered horribly at the hands of their respected peers. My very effective disciplining method had morphed into humiliation and torture. Nothing could be worse than being associated with me, the source of all their degradation, shame, and catastrophic embarrassment. They would have preferred a dagger to the heart over the utter disgrace those words induced.

This happened to them outside of school as well. If they saw a friend, who was a student of mine, at the mall, the park, or restaurant, those aversive three words would inevitably fly off their lips, leaving my poor daughters recoiling in horror, wincing in psychological pain, and worrying about their heretofore hard-earned social status. This horrid expression seemed to follow them everywhere. Their only safe haven was their room at home—that is, until the phone rang and one of their friends was on the line ready to deliver the dirty three-word trio upon their wounded psyche. Okay, maybe I'm exaggerating again. All I know is that both my daughters made it crystal clear to me that I said "Oops, off task" a few too many times in class.

Today, as adults, they can simply look back and laugh. Yet even now, when they happen to run into past middle school friends, it's evident that the thing these friends remember most about Mr. Wong is not his engaging assignments, riveting lectures, or stimulating personality. It's not his way of making hard concepts understandable or his effective motivation methods. It wasn't that they learned a lot of useful lessons that positively affected their lives. Nope, it was none of these things. That's right, you guessed it. It was "Oops, off task!"

Chapter 22

Student Impact

Teacher: Where's your homework?
Student: I lost it fighting a kid who said you weren't the best teacher in school.

Here is a wonderful, thought-provoking episode of *The Twilight Zone* from 1962 that would resonate with any teacher. It's called "The Changing of the Guard" and is about an aging literature teacher at an all-boys school who loves his job. Unfortunately, he learns his contract will not be renewed, due to old age, and he is initially shocked and dismayed. He then quickly becomes depressed as he convinces himself his entire career was worthless, pointless, and unrewarding. He surmises that his students did not learn anything from him. They took away absolutely nothing important from his class, and his lessons were insignificant, boring, and forgettable. He reflects on his lengthy fifty-year teaching career and sees nothing of value. He's been a failure. He has not positively impacted any student, and his entire life has been purposeless, meaningless, and hollow.

This kind of nightmarish thinking crosses the minds of all teachers, at one time or another. All teachers hope and believe they are making a positive difference in their students' lives. Maybe we taught them something that helped them in college or on their jobs. Maybe the relationship we developed with our students helped them cope with some of their own troubling life situations. Maybe we gave them some advice that actually worked! Since most teachers choose teaching so they can "touch the future," it's devastating to conclude you have failed in this endeavor, whether you have taught for only a few years or are retired after a thirty-four-year career.

In fact, teachers like to fantasize about former students being successful and their role in that success. Imagine having a past student who ended up becoming president of the United States. This is the ultimate fantasy. Let's say you had this person in eighth grade language arts class many, many years ago, and the reading, writing, and speaking skills you taught him (or her) helped (or were crucial!) on his road to the presidency. You'd see him on TV and comment to your spouse about how you *knew* he was special at the age of fourteen and imply a specific lesson where he learned something from you.

(excitedly) "Hey, honey! Did you hear that word the president just used?" while listening to his State of the Union Address on TV.

"Huh, no, I mean, which word are you referring to?"

"He just said *encompassing*. That was a word I had on my monthly vocabulary list in eighth grade. I taught him that word!"

Few teachers can claim the privilege of having a president as a past student. And if you can, you were probably in the private sector. Nevertheless, teachers need to know we made some sort of difference, large or small. I've had many students over the years who thanked me or told me how interesting a lesson was or even related something they learned from my class that came in handy later. This is always wonderful to hear, since it's like a spiritual injection. For a while, afterward, there's an elated skip in my step and a renewed motivation to my teaching. You *want* to believe those students are telling you the truth, yet there is also the reality that the student has a hidden agenda.

For instance, I'm positive that these kinds of complimentary statements often come from a desire to, for lack of a better phrase, "suck up" to the teacher. No matter how hard a teacher tries to be fair to all students, the human condition dictates that nice and cooperative (and complimentary) students will be related to in a more positive way. Students who do nothing but give the teacher shit will find themselves receiving no breaks or benefits of the doubt. It's a normal reaction. So some students have figured this out. Being nice may get them the desired outcome, whether it's preferential seating, a hall pass, more time to complete the assignment, or even a better grade. And to tell you the truth, this is a lesson in life that will definitely pay dividends in their future. Just being nice, whether you are faking it or not, is a necessary characteristic of success.

So there's always this nagging idea in the back of teachers' heads that entertain the possibility of failure, and it can hurt. But let's get back to the ending of that *Twilight Zone* episode. Remember the old teacher was depressed over his presumed failure at reaching his students. The episode continues with him on the verge of suicide when he goes to his empty classroom to gather up his personal items. He's at his desk with his head down. Suddenly, he looks up to discover his desks filled with past students, students who had already died. They were ghosts who had returned to tell him something. One student thanked him for teaching him about courage and quoted from a specific poem the teacher had read in class. The teacher then recalls that this student had died in World War II, trying to save his comrades from enemy fire, and had been awarded the Congressional Medal of Honor posthumously. Another student, who had died in a car accident, thanked him for allowing him to live a happy and fulfilling life, by teaching him the meaning of true love. He referred to a work of literature discussed in his class and the connection to this and his joyous twenty-year marriage. One after another, the ghost students declare their indebtedness and appreciation for what they learned in his class and how it made their lives better. All of this was previously unknown to the aging teacher, and only through the magic of visiting the "twilight zone" is this truth realized. The students then disappear, leaving the teacher with an entirely different life perspective. The episode ends with the teacher content and ready for his retirement years.

For any teacher who ever wonders about the impact you have made on your students, please watch this episode. It's actually frightfully scary until the end, when the old teacher is more than satisfied with the mark he has left on his students. And the message is so true! A teacher may never have actual proof of this, but the difference you make is inevitable. The mere fact that students successfully pass the next grade level is indicative of the teacher's effectiveness, let alone embracing some concept like courage or love.

Teaching, in some ways, is like being a dentist. And I don't mean it's like pulling a tooth to get students to work! But I read somewhere that, of all the occupations out there, dentistry tended to be correlated with a high rate of suicide. I guess it may have had something to do with mercury poisoning affecting their mental state. I don't think dentists use mercury very much anymore, and thank God, mercury isn't a common element in America's classrooms. Now, I'm not sure where teachers are on the suicide list, but the reasoning with dentists (other than the mercury theory) is that they have a tough job, and nobody likes to see them. In fact, most of us hate going to a dentist, and dentists can sense this, even if the patient does not articulate it. Also, and more importantly, dentists rarely have a chance to admire their work or relish in their achievements. Conversely, a construction worker can point to a building and say, "Hey, look at that thing of beauty, and I built that!" A salesman can pull out a piece of data from the computer and declare, "Wow, I sold thirty-five cars this month!" An artist can simply show his paintings, and a waiter can beam at the tips he is getting. But a dentist cannot, while walking down the street with a friend, see a patient and approach him with a request to open his mouth so that his friend can gloat over the artistry of a filled cavity. In fact, the patient, upon seeing his dentist randomly and unsuspectedly in public, may start running in the opposite direction! Just kidding, of course. That would never happen.

Likewise, a teacher does not see the "fruits of his or her labor" as often as they need to. But know that it is there. And the phrase "fruits of labor" does not refer to salary, which is one of the lowest for an occupation that requires a college degree. The fruit of a teacher's labor is knowing the time spent in the classroom provided students with useful lessons that enhanced their lives.

Chapter 23

Thank Goodness
for Teaching!

*Choose a job you love, and you'll never have to
work a day in your life.*

—Confucius

The only skill in life I have is teaching. I can't fix anything, computers are confusing to me, and I possess zero construction knowledge. I remember, a number of years ago, I tried to help an extended family member build his house. On one day I was there, he was doing some electrical wiring. He dutifully and patiently showed me how to connect the wires from the wall socket into the electrical switch. The black wire goes here, the red one here, then you shove it in, and screw it to the wall. I was doing fine for a short while, but it became boring, and I ended up making a few mistakes. Later that day, he went around to test the outlets. Unfortunately, a few caused his tester to explode. Even with this blunder under my belt, he actually asked me to help him on another day. This time it was roofing. Once again, he calmly explained the simplicity of hammering composition tiles to the roof and then descended down the ladder to attend to work inside the house. About an hour later, he made his way up the ladder to inspect my work. He started looking at it, hesitated, and then began pulling about half my tiles from the roof and tossing them to the ground. Somehow I messed it up, so the rest of the day, I carried two-by-fours from point A to point B, a task that was almost impossible to screw up.

So throughout my adult life, I have depended on others to complete what most males would label simple projects, like changing a light fixture, mounting a towel rack, or installing a ceiling fan. Okay, please stop laughing. It's true. I can't do these things even if I tried my hardest. And if I dared attempt these tasks, I'd screw it up, thus causing more damage, work, and money to fix it. And I'd probably sustain an injury as well.

Furthermore, I know nothing in the area you might call "mechanical." Gas engines baffle me. I never had the experience of "working on cars," like a lot of my male friends did. The whole thing is just a jumbled mess of confusion. The farthest I ever progressed in this area was to change the oil in one of my cars when I was nineteen. Today, however, it just seems easier and safer for me to have Jiffy Lube do it rather than take the chance of messing it up or breaking something.

But what about computers? Same thing. This is another perplexing phenomena. It just seems like there's a lot of illogical nonsense when trying to navigate your way using your personal computer. I can follow instructions perfectly well, but with the frequency of change when it comes to computers, following instructions becomes a moot point. As soon as the format is changed, I get frustrated. I just got used to the old format, damn it! Yes, I do use e-mail, I sometimes surf the net, and I know the basics of Word. Other than that, the computer might as well be a gas engine.

Also, I've lived in an area of the country my entire life that has superb fishing, camping, hunting, hiking, and boating venues, yet I know almost nothing about these activities. I'd like to think it's my parents' fault, who never exposed me to these things. We weren't particularly poor, but these activities cost more money than throwing us kids a basketball or football. Thus, I never had an opportunity to know them, or like them, and this carried over to my adult life. Anyway, I can remember many conversations with friends who were expounding about their cool camping trip, naming hiking trails in the area, or talking about fishing or boating equipment—all of which were foreign to me.

All I could do was to pretend I knew what they were talking about, smile, and nod my head in confirmation. Okay, maybe I'm too hard on myself. I do know a lot about education and teaching and certain specific sports. In this complicated world, that might be all anyone can be expected to know. *All* of us are smart in some areas and in academic need in many others. I'll bet Bill Gates wouldn't know where to begin if someone asked him to perform a radiator flush in his Porsche. If Bill Clinton was asked who won the Super Bowl last year and, for extra credit, name the quarterback, he'd certainly scratch his head and blush with embarrassment. And try asking Stephen Hawking about the specifications of a Harley-Davidson 883 Sportster, and he might sway you quickly into a conversation about how the universe was formed. So it's really a specialized world we live in. Nowadays, very intelligent people depend on others to do for them what others would see as very simple tasks. That's just the way it is. Okay, I feel better about myself now.

Anyway, my point is that I'm so pleased I was able to find my niche in life—teaching—since I don't seem to be very skilled at anything else. I can talk about teaching all day, and when you are with a group of teachers, that's usually what happens, much to the dismay of their nonteaching spouses. I feel very lucky to have discovered, or stumbled into, such a rewarding and semirespected profession.

Chapter 24

Any Questions?

A father and young son went fishing, and the boy became curious about things and started asking all sorts of questions.

"Dad, why does the boat float?"

The father replied, "Don't rightly know, son."

A little later, the boy asked, "How do fish breathe underwater?"

"Don't rightly know," replied the father again.

"Why is the sky blue?" said the boy.

"Don't know the answer to that one either, my son," replied the father.

Finally, the boy asked, "Dad, do you mind me asking you all these questions?"

The father replied, "Of course not. If you don't ask questions, you'll never learn anything."

or some unknown reason, people who have read my book, especially current or former teachers, have questions about some of the stuff they read. So here are the most common questions followed by my most humble and honest answers:

1. You've talked about some of the bizarre happenings you have experienced in public schools. Did you leave any out? Are there others?

Well, there were many, actually. Another one that sticks out in my mind, however, occurred over a period of about six months. What happened was that the teachers and students would discover a dump in the middle of the upstairs hallway about twice a week. Someone, or something, had taken a shit in the middle of the hallway at the middle school where I taught.

We ruled out an errant animal. That might explain one time when a large lost dog, confused deer, or freaked-out raccoon might inexplicably find itself on the second floor of the school, and inadvertently be startled, thus leaving an unintentional offering to mark its previous presence. But these piles of fecal matter were consistent, in time, place, and form. We had on our hands a very regular student doing his routine very regularly.

This occurred in the 1990s, and our school had no operating cameras that might easily catch the culprit. Instead, teachers in the hallway, where the dirty deeds were done, would stick their heads out of their classroom doors at unexpected, unpredictable times hoping to surprise the "mad crapper," as we so affectionately named him.

But no one was ever observed in such a precarious position, and the poopy findings suddenly stopped. We never found out who was responsible for this most unusual behavior. The custodian was very much relieved to not get any more calls about a cleanup on the second-floor hallway.

2. All teachers have students who have misbehaved, and you mentioned a few of yours. Did you deal with any other particularly bad students?

Not really. I never had any student physically attack me, like some of my colleagues experienced. I had many passive-aggressive students, though. These students would quietly not follow instructions. They wouldn't yell, or have a fit, or get violent. They would simply refuse to cooperate, and stay calm about it, or even polite about it.

I had a female student who refused to follow the "no gum chewing" rule. Now, this was a schoolwide rule written in the school handbook. I agree that this isn't the worst behavior a student might exhibit, but it was a rule that the teachers were expected to enforce.

Anyway, she came to my class chewing gum *every* day. The first few times, I simply asked her to spit out her gum, hoping she would get the hint. But it didn't work. The next few times, I told her that she had lost "points," which would negatively impact her grade, and she would have to make up the points by doing extra credit. This didn't work either.

So the next few times, I gave her "lunch cleanups." This is where she had to sacrifice the last ten minutes of her lunch period by grabbing a sponge and cleaning off lunch tables. This wasn't enough incentive either.

The next step in my progressive consequences mode of operandi was to give her "after-school detentions." This is where the student must stay after school for seventy-five minutes in a detention room. So this is what she received the next few times she came to class chewing gum, but this also wasn't enough to stop her from chewing gum.

Finally, my last option was to write an "office referral." This meant I filled out an office referral form explaining the infraction, and the student would visit the vice principal's office for appropriate consequences. Office referrals were reserved for the most serious offenses.

When she was called down to the VP's office, the VP was a little perturbed with *me*. Why was I sending a student to her for such a minor offense? Evidently, she hadn't fully read my referral; otherwise, she would have known that this was *not* the first, or second, or even third time this student had broken the chewing gum rule, but rather the thirteenth time in a row. Anyway, a meeting with the student, the VP, and myself was believed, by the VP, to solve the problem.

So the next day, I was called down to the VP's office, where the student was patiently seated, a smile on her face, content with her passive-aggressive self, while lounging on one of the VP's most comfortable chairs. Once again, the VP asked me to explain why I wrote an office referral for a student who was simply chewing gum. So I started my explanation, but suddenly, some familiar movement caught the corner of my eye. I turned slightly and saw the student delightedly chomping on some gum.

3. It sounds like you had a principal who was very effective and well liked when you taught at a middle school. Did you work for many ineffective principals?

Yes. Most of the principals I worked for were ineffective in at least one area, or more. He or she may excel at one or two skills but lack other necessary attributes to do the job well. For example, I worked for a principal who trusted the teachers to make good classroom decisions but always sided with the complaining parent. He was easy to get along with but had no "backbone," which meant he never seemed to make the tough decisions until it was too late.

Being a principal is unmistakably a demanding, difficult job. I could not do it. There are very few who can do the job well. So when you come across a principal who is really effective in all areas, it's quite a pleasure to work for him. And the only principal that fits that description is the one you referred to in your question. I don't think he would mind me mentioning his real name—Jim Noddings.

4. You said you started teaching in 1979 and retired in 2013. How has teaching changed over time?

It seems like most of the changes are a result of new technology in schools. For example, I started out putting student grades in a green paper gradebook with a pencil and then using a calculator to figure out final, individual grades. Now, of course, it's all done on the computer, and you can press a key to generate anything you want— from a flowchart showing a student's worst to best score, to the mean, median, and mode of the student's reading assignments only.

In 1979, copies of worksheets were done on mimeograph machines. I can still vividly recall the smell of the ink. The first thing the students did when receiving their copy was to put their nose to the sheet and inhale. A scene from the movie *Fast Times at Ridgemont High* shows thirty students doing this simultaneously upon receiving their handouts. Now, the school has printers that can crank out a hundred plus copies a minute, and some teachers have individual printers in their own rooms.

I started out with a blackboard and white chalk. Colored chalk was considered pretty cool stuff. Now the computerized front boards can do pretty much anything, without getting your hands dirty.

In 1979, school and faculty lunches were good, in my opinion. Real mashed potatoes with turkey gravy, slices of chocolate swirl ice cream, and meat loaf to die for still makes my mouth water. Yum! Today's students get "healthy" foods, such as uncooked broccoli, fat-free milk, and a full salad bar. These foods are largely ignored by the students who hone in on the pizza and cheeseburgers.

It seems schools were much safer in 1979. Kids walked to school through the woods; getting bullied was an individual weakness; teachers weren't grooming and fucking his or her students, and students weren't bringing guns to school. Or is it just that these things existed but weren't reported, like today?

But one of the biggest differences concerns the lack of trust for teachers. In 1979, the principal, the parents, and the whole community trusted the teachers to make the right decisions in the classroom. The teachers felt like professionals who were respected and expected to improve the student's academic and social skills. They were, for the most part, left alone to do the job they knew well. Now, this trust is sorrowfully lacking. Teachers are getting way too many messages that eat away at the trust they once had. Teachers are made to feel like it's their fault if a student fails, never mind the student's socioeconomic status, language abilities, or family problems. It's really sad. In my opinion, today's younger teachers are actually more prepared and more enthusiastic about teaching compared to 1979. This makes this lack of trust issue even more ridiculous. I really hope the pendulum starts swinging back to 1979 before there is a real teaching crisis.

In 1979, students communicated with other students by passing notes. Today, they text, and it's much more difficult for a teacher to catch a student texting. Just because a student has his head tilted down smiling at his crotch doesn't prove he's texting.

5. What things have remained the same?

The salary for teachers is still low. No change here. For a profession that requires a college degree, it's still one of the lowest-paid occupations.

The school building and facilities have remained in pretty good shape throughout the years, in my experience. Consistent remodeling and upgrading of schools is something that takes place in most school districts. I realize there are many places in America where this doesn't occur. Once again, I've been pretty lucky.

Whether it's 1979 or today, students and teachers love snow days!

And lastly, I believe students are basically the same. They are confused, sexually wired, random, and funny creatures. Most mean well and try pretty hard. They are still in need of direction and guidance but want to make the most of their lives, even if it means failing to write that short story for Mr. Wong. They are resilient, tough, and persevere through some of the most unimaginable living conditions. Students are still the future of this country, and the mark teachers make on their lives will determine America's continued success.

6. Are you glad you retired when you did?

Yes.

7. Any regrets?

Absolutely none.

Epilogue

A man's got to take a lot of punishment
to write a funny book.

—Ernest Hemingway

There you have it! My odyssey. My educational escapades. My career adventure laid bare before your eyes—my life! I have succeeded in disrespecting every element of public education, making fun of every teacher, administrator, and student I have ever come in contact with. I have embarrassed the profession as a whole and have jeopardized all the hard work educators have labored over thus far to improve the system. I have ridiculed my colleagues and lampooned all that is sacred about the profession. I have made a mockery of teaching, and made myself, in particular, appear to be the town idiot. Furthermore, I imparted to you *way* too much degrading, personal information about me, my family, and friends.

And I hope you enjoyed it.

About the Author

Roger Wong lived most of his life in the greater Seattle area, with the exception of a three-year stint in the US Army (1972–1975) where he served in Germany protecting America and our European allies against those nasty Russian commies. He currently lives with his wife, Jean, and her annoying cat. He's enjoying retirement by traveling, working out, reading, and watching football and baseball games on TV with his neighbor.

Roger's wife is currently teaching, so Roger's new occupation of "house manager" keeps him busy with laundry, cooking, paying bills, cleaning, and yard work. He's been fortunate that there haven't been too many "misadventures" involved with managing the house.

With the current public school emphasis on overtesting students, blaming teachers for all student failures, a deterioration of professional respect, and misguided reforms, Roger hopes the educational pendulum will swing back to better times, for the sake of his daughter, who is just beginning her journey as a new teacher, and for all those hardworking, dedicated teachers across America.

CPSIA information can be obtained
at www.ICGtesting.com
Printed in the USA
LVOW12s0529260416

485339LV00001B/53/P